**MEDICAL**

# HIGH-YIELD WORKBOOK

ISBN: 978-1-62523-427-8

# AUTHORS

**Steven R. Harris, Ph.D.**
Associate Dean for Academic Affairs
Professor of Pharmacology
Kentucky College of Osteopathic Medicine
Pikeville, KY

**John Kriak, Pharm.D.**
Educational Consultant
Johnstown, PA

**Michael Manley, M.D.**
Department of Neurosciences
University of California, San Diego

Senior Director, Step 1 Curriculum,
Kaplan Medical
Los Angeles, CA

**Kim Moscatello, Ph.D.**
Professor of Microbiology and Immunology
Lake Erie College of Osteopathic Medicine
Erie, PA

**Sam Turco, Ph.D.**
Professor, Department of Biochemistry
University of Kentucky College of Medicine
Lexington, KY

**James White, Ph.D.**
Assistant Professor of Cell Biology
School of Osteopathic Medicine, University
  of Medicine and Dentistry of New Jersey

Adjunct Assistant Professor of Cell and
  Developmental Biology
University of Pennsylvania School of Medicine
Philadelphia, PA

**L. Britt Wilson, Ph.D.**
Associate Professor, Department of
  Pharmacology, Physiology, and Neuroscience
University of S. Carolina School of Medicine
Columbia, SC

# CONTRIBUTORS

**John Barone, M.D.**
Anatomic and Clinical Pathology
Private Practice
Los Angeles, CA

**Charles Faselis, M.D.**
Chairman of Medicine
VA Medical Center

Associate Professor of Medicine
George Washington University
School of Medicine
Washington, DC

**Alina Gonzalez-Mayo, M.D.**
Psychiatrist
Department of Veteran's Administration
Bay Pines, FL

**Nancy Standler, M.D., Ph.D.**
Department of Pathology
Valley View Medical Center,
Intermountain Health Care
Cedar City, UT

# CONTENTS

## PART II: ORGAN SYSTEMS

# General Principles

# Part I

# BIOCHEMISTRY

## TOPIC 1: MOLECULAR BIOLOGY I

1.  The various features of the bases found in DNA or RNA are shown below. Complete the table by filling in the empty cells.

| Base | Nucleoside | Nucleotide in Nucleic Acids |
|---|---|---|
| | Adenosine (deoxyadenosine) | dAMP, AMP |
| Guanine | | dGMP, GMP |
| Cytosine | | dCMP, CMP |
| Uracil | Uridine (deoxyuridine) | |
| Thymine | | |

2.  Two structural differences between DNA and RNA are:

3.  A major assumption that must be made if a single strand of DNA or RNA sequence is shown and no orientation of the sequence is given is _____.

4. The difference between 10 nm and 30 nm chromatin is _____.

5. In which intra-nuclear area (euchromatin, heterochromatin, or nucleolus) are the following RNAs synthesized?

   mRNA _____

   tRNA _____

   rRNA _____

6. An oncologist is conducting a study of specific gene mutations that are hypothesized to increase the risk for developing breast cancer. Women who were shown to be positive for specific variations in the BRCA-1 and BRCA-2 gene sequence were further screened for sequence variations in other associated genes. Interestingly, the following gene sequence identified from exon 1 of the androgen receptor (AR) gene was found to have a high degree of heterogeneity between individuals with breast cancer: 5'-TTCATCATCATCATCATCATCATCATCC-3'. An increased length in this sequence was reportedly associated with increased incidence of breast cancer in BRCA-1 mutation carriers. During which phase of the cell cycle were these variations most likely generated?

   (A)  $G_0$
   (B)  $G_1$
   (C)  $G_2$
   (D)  M
   (E)  S

7. In DNA replication in prokaryotes and eukaryotes, 5'-exonuclease performs the function of _____ whereas the 3'-exonuclease performs the function of

   _____.

8. An important class of antimicrobials that is used to inhibit DNA replication in prokaryotes is _____, which inhibit the enzyme _____.

9. _____ are the DNA sequences present at the ends of eukaryotic chromosomes. _____ is the enzyme present in eukaryotes, but not prokaryotes, which is involved in _____ .

10. A drug targeted to inhibit telomerase would be useful to treat the _____ disease state.

11. For each cell type below, indicate the relative telomerase activity (high or low) found in each cell, and briefly discuss the biological ramifications of that level of telomerase activity for each cell.

Embryonic cell:

Normal adult cell:

Tumor cell:

12. The various features of the DNA repair mechanism are shown below. Complete the table by filling in the empty cells.

| DNA Repair | Example | Key Enzyme(s) | Clinical Relationship | Phase of Cell Cycle |
|---|---|---|---|---|
| **Thymine dimer** | UV radiation | | | |
| **Mismatch base** | DNA replication errors | | | $G_2$ |
| **Base excision** | | Uracil glycosylase, AP endonuclease | None | |

13. In RNA transcription, RNA polymerase first recognizes and binds to a region of DNA called
_____. Then the enzyme reads the strand of the double-stranded gene
called the _____ in a _____ direction. The strand of the
gene that is not read by RNA polymerase is called the _____.

14. An important antimicrobial that is used to inhibit transcription in prokaryotes is
_____, which inhibits the enzyme _____.
The toxic substance in poisonous mushrooms that inhibits RNA transcription in eukaryotes is
_____, which inhibits the enzyme _____.
_____ inhibits transcription in both prokaryotes and eukaryotes.

15. Two major similarities between DNA polymerase and RNA polymerase are:

16. Two major differences between DNA polymerase and RNA polymerase are:

17. During replication, the DNA template sequence CTGTA would replicate to produce the sequence
_____.

18. During transcription, the DNA template sequence CTGTA would transcribe to produce
_____.

19. In systemic lupus erythematosus, autoantibodies are directed against which of the following?

    (A)   7-methyl-G cap of mRNA

    (B)   Spliceosomes

    (C)   Modified bases of tRNA

    (D)   rRNA of the ribosome

    (E)   Poly A tails of mRNA

20. Even though there are approximately 3 billion bases per haploid genome, only about 1.5% of the genome actually encodes for genes. Explain why chromosomal DNA is mostly non-coding DNA.

21. Even though improper splicing out of introns is the source of many diseases, what is the main advantage of introns in genes?

22. In prokaryotic ribosomes, the small subunit size is _____ and the large subunit size is _____ and together equal _____. In eukaryotic ribosomes, the small sub-unit size is _____ and the large subunit size is _____ and together equal _____.

23. tRNAs are the smallest of the RNAs and have a cloverleaf structure in which the amino acid is attached to the tRNA at the 3' end of the sequence _____.

24. Describe a mechanism by which a gene in human cells could be expressed in 2 different forms, one that is translated on free ribosomes and remains in the cytoplasm, and a second form that is secreted from the cell. Assume that the mechanism is related to the expression steps for this gene and does not involve any alteration in the translation or secretory machinery of the cell.

25. Using the genetic code below, what is the amino acid sequence encoded by the following DNA sequence?

........ATGTTTGCGAAACAG......

_____

| First Position (5' End) | Second Position | | | | Third Position (3' End) |
|---|---|---|---|---|---|
| | **U** | **C** | **A** | **G** | |
| **U** | UUU ⎱Phe<br>UUC ⎰<br>UUA ⎱Leu<br>UUG ⎰ | UCU ⎱<br>UCC ⎱Ser<br>UCA ⎰<br>UCG ⎰ | UAU ⎱Tyr<br>UAC ⎰<br>UAA ⎱Stop<br>UAG ⎰ | UGU ⎱Cys<br>UGC ⎰<br>UGA   Stop<br>UGG   Trp | U<br>C<br>A<br>G |
| **C** | CUU ⎱<br>CUC ⎱Leu<br>CUA ⎰<br>CUG ⎰ | CCU ⎱<br>CCC ⎱Pro<br>CCA ⎰<br>CCG ⎰ | CAU ⎱His<br>CAC ⎰<br>CAA ⎱Gln<br>CAG ⎰ | CGU ⎱<br>CGC ⎱Arg<br>CGA ⎰<br>CGG ⎰ | U<br>C<br>A<br>G |
| **A** | AUU ⎱<br>AUC ⎱Ile<br>AUA ⎰<br>AUG   Met | ACU ⎱<br>ACC ⎱Thr<br>ACA ⎰<br>ACG ⎰ | AAU ⎱Asn<br>AAC ⎰<br>AAA ⎱Lys<br>AAG ⎰ | AGU ⎱Ser<br>AGC ⎰<br>AGA ⎱Arg<br>AGG ⎰ | U<br>C<br>A<br>G |
| **G** | GUU ⎱<br>GUC ⎱Val<br>GUA ⎰<br>GUG ⎰ | GCU ⎱<br>GCC ⎱Ala<br>GCA ⎰<br>GCG ⎰ | GAU ⎱Asp<br>GAC ⎰<br>GAA ⎱Glu<br>GAG ⎰ | GGU ⎱<br>GGC ⎱Gly<br>GGA ⎰<br>GGG ⎰ | U<br>C<br>A<br>G |

26. DNA sequence surrounding the beginning of the 5'-exon of a gene is as shown below:

    **........GG ATG TTT GCG TC̲G......**

    Suppose a mutation resulted in the C (underlined) being converted to an (A) This kind of mutation is called _____.

27. What would be the sequence of an anticodon that would bind to the codon transcribed from the trinucleotide CAG in the template strand of the gene?

28. A summary of important antibiotics that inhibit translation in prokaryotes is shown below. List the site of action of the respective antibiotic and the consequence in translation.

| Antibiotic | Site of Action and Consequence |
|---|---|
| Chloramphenicol | |
| Clindamycin | |
| Erythromycin | |
| Neomycin | |
| Tetracycline | |

29. A 53-year-old man comes to his physician with complaints of strange movements and behavior changes for the past 2 months. His wife states that the patient has progressively become socially withdrawn, inattentive, uncharacteristically aggressive, and irritable. Physical examination shows irregular, sudden, jerky movements of both legs and arms that sometimes awaken the patient at night. Expansion of which of the following sequences is associated with this man's condition?

    (A)   5'-AAAAAAAAAAAA-3'

    (B)   5'-CAGCAGCAGCAG-3'

    (C)   5'-CAGGACCAGGAC-3'

    (D)   5'-GGGCCCGGGCCC-3'

    (E)   5'-GGGGGGGGGGGG-3'

30. Define the protein structures below and list an example.

| Protein Structure | Definition | Example |
|---|---|---|
| Primary | | |
| Secondary | | |
| Tertiary | | |
| Quaternary | | |

31. What are 2 reasons why a protein misfolds?

32. Concisely explain how misfolded proteins are handled in the cytoplasm of cells.

33. What determines whether a protein will be secreted or remain in the cytoplasm of a cell?

34. N-glycosylation of proteins occurs in the _____ (intracellular location) in the cell. An example of a protein that is N-glycosylated is _____.
O-glycosylation of proteins occurs in the _____ (intracellular location) in the cell. An example of a protein that is O-glycosylated is _____.

35. List whether the respective protein modification is co-translational, post-translational, or both.

| Modification | Co-Translational, Post-Translational, or Both? |
| --- | --- |
| Disulfide bond formation | |
| Proteolysis | |
| Phosphorylation | |
| Gamma-carboxylation | |
| Prenylation | |
| O-glycosylation | |
| N-glycosylation | |

36. I-cell disease is most often due to a defect in the enzyme _____, which functions to _____. The result of the catalytic function of the normal enzyme enables lysosomal enzymes to enter the lysosome of a cell. Another situation that could give rise to I-cell disease is a defect in _____.

37. Why do cells from patients with I-cell disease have inclusion bodies?

38. While the collagen superfamily of proteins includes more than 25 collagen types, the most important types for the exam are shown below. Complete the table by filling in the blank cells.

| Collagen Type | Characteristics | Tissue Distribution | Associated Diseases |
|---|---|---|---|
| I | | | |
| II | Thin fibrils; structural | | |
| III | Thin fibrils; pliable | | |
| IV | Amorphous | | |

39. Place the following steps in collagen synthesis in the proper sequential order.

_____ Triple helix formation

_____ Removal of the hydrophobic signal sequence

_____ Oxidation by lysyl oxidase that requires $O_2$ and copper

_____ Glycosylation of selected hydroxylysines

_____ Aggregation to form the fibril

_____ Enzymatic removal of N- and C-terminal peptides

_____ Enzymatic activity by 2 enzymes that require vitamin C

_____ Secretion of the protein from the cell

40. The major organelles and macrostructures in a cell are shown below. Complete the table by filling in the empty cells.

| Organelle and Macrostructure | Structural Features | Main Function(s) |
|---|---|---|
| Mitochondrion | | |
| Peroxisome | | |
| Smooth endoplasmic reticulum | | |
| Rough endoplasmic reticulum | | |
| Golgi apparatus | | |
| Nucleus | Double membrane compartment | |
| Lysosome | | |
| Vacuole | Single membrane compartment | |
| Cilia | Microtubule protein | |

41. _____ is the name of the ATPase motor molecule involved in anterograde transport on microtubules, and _____ is involved in retrograde transport on microtubules. _____ and _____ are examples of drugs that inhibit microtubule assembly.

42. _____ is the name of the genetic disease that involves a microtubule polymerization defect, impairing fusion of phagosomes and lysosomes. A key feature of this disease is _____.

43. _____ is the name of the genetic disease that involves immotile cilia and infertility due to immotile spermatozoa.

# TOPIC 2: MOLECULAR BIOLOGY II

1. Several major specific transcription factors are shown below. Complete the table by filling in the empty cells.

| Name | Response Element | Function | Protein Class |
|---|---|---|---|
| **Steroid receptors** | | Response to steroids | |
| **CREB** | | | |
| **PPARs** | | | |
| **NF = κB** | κB elements | | Rel domains |
| **Homeodomain proteins** | | | Helix-turn-helix |

2. A child is brought to the university hospital with severe birth defects, including limb abnormalities, congenital deafness, and pigment abnormalities. Which of the following genes or DNA sequences is most likely mutated in this individual?

(A) CCAAT box within an enhancer

(B) PAX gene

(C) RAS gene

(D) Tyrosine hydroxylase gene

(E) UPE GC-rich sequence within an enhancer

3.  Extracellular estrogen initiates a series of steps by a cell. These steps constitute a signaling pathway. List these steps (that is, how does estrogen give a signal to a cell?).

    Imagine that cells could be cultured in sodium chloride, potassium, calcium, and magnesium only. How would this impact estrogen signaling?

    Post-menopausal women with breast cancer can often be successfully treated with estrogen or related compounds. In one such patient, a clinical response of several years ended when her cancer relapsed. List 3 possible explanations for how her tumor became resistant to estrogen therapy.

4.  The major differences between genomic and cDNA libraries are shown below. Complete the table by filling in the empty cells.

| | Genomic Libraries | cDNA Libraries |
|---|---|---|
| **Source of DNA** | | mRNA (cDNA) |
| **Key enzymes to make library** | | |
| **Contains nonexpressed sequences of chromosomes** | Yes | |
| **Cloned genes are complete sequences** | Not necessarily | |
| **Cloned genes contain introns** | | |
| **Promoter and enhancer sequences present** | Yes, but not necessarily in same clone | |
| **Gene can be expressed in cloning host** | | |
| **Gene can be used for gene therapy or transgenics** | | Yes |

5.  Cloning of a new eukaryotic gene was followed by insertion and ligation of the gene into an expression vector. The protein translated from this gene was then studied on a western blot and probed with $^{32}$P-DNA, yielding a positive result. These findings eliminate which of the following substances as a candidate for the likely gene product?

    (A) CREB

    (B) Protein kinase A

    (C) RNA polymerase

    (D) PPAR

    (E) Steroid receptor

6. Several types of commonly used blots are shown below. Complete the table by filling in the empty cells.

| Name | Material Analyzed | Electrophoresis Required | Probe | Purpose |
|------|-------------------|--------------------------|-------|---------|
| Southern | | Yes | | |
| Northern | | | | |
| Western | | | | |
| Dot | RNA, DNA, protein | | Same as above | Detects RNA, DNA, or proteins |

7. An HIV-positive woman who has been on combination therapy for 8 years goes to her physician with no complaints. Her blood work shows a steadily decreasing CD4 count. Physical examination reveals generalized lymphadenopathy, and she is diagnosed with cervical dysplasia. The physician wants to check her viral load before changing her treatment regimen. Which of the following tests should he use?

(A) ELISA for the p24 antibody

(B) HIV culture with antigen detection

(C) HIV DNA polymerase chain reaction (PCR)

(D) HIV reverse transcriptase-PCR

(E) Western blot for HIV-specific antibodies

# TOPIC 3: MEDICAL GENETICS

1.  Define the terms below.

| | Definition |
|---|---|
| **Gene** | |
| **Locus** | |
| **Allele** | |
| **Haploid** | |
| **Somatic cell** | |
| **Gametes** | |
| **Polymorphism** | |
| **Genotype** | |
| **Phenotype** | |
| **Loss of function mutation** | |
| **Gain of function mutation** | |
| **Recurrence risk** | |
| **Punnett square** | |

2.  If a pedigree shows that the disease trait has a vertical appearance and the disease is in every generation, the mode of inheritance is dominant or recessive (*circle one*).

3.  If a pedigree shows that the disease trait has a horizontal appearance and the disease skips a generation, the mode of inheritance is dominant or recessive (*circle one*).

4.  If a pedigree shows that the disease trait has male-to-male transmission, the mode of inheritance is autosomal or X-linked (*circle one*).

5.  If a pedigree shows that the disease trait does not have male-to-male transmission, the mode of inheritance is autosomal or X-linked (*circle one*).

6.  What is the main distinguishing characteristic of mitochondrial mode of inheritance?

7.  For each of the pedigrees below, state the mode of inheritance:

| | Mode of Inheritance |
|---|---|
| | |
| | |
| | |
| | |
| | |

8. Listed below are factors that influence phenotypic expression in single gene disorders. Define the term and state a disease example of each.

| Term | Definition | Disease Example |
|---|---|---|
| Environmental factors | | |
| Allelic heterogeneity | | |
| Incomplete penetrance | | |
| Variable expression | | |
| Pleiotropy | | |
| Locus heterogeneity | | |
| Anticipation | | |
| Imprinting | | |
| Uniparental disomy | | |

9. The most common type of Prader-Willi syndrome involves a loss of genetic material on the

_____ chromosome, which was inherited from the _____ parent. The

corresponding genetic material inherited from the other parent is transcriptionally inactive due

to _____. The more rare type of Prader-Willi syndrome involves a child who inherits 2

copies of chromosome _____ from which parent? _____

10. The most common type of Angelman's syndrome involves a loss of genetic material on the

_____ chromosome, which was inherited from the _____ parent. The

corresponding genetic material inherited from the other parent is transcriptionally inactive due

to _____. The more rare type of Angelman's syndrome involves a child who inherits 2

copies of chromosome _____ from which parent? _____

11. What is the definition of genotype frequency?

12. What is the definition of allele frequency?

13. By convention, allele frequency is p + q = 1, where p is _____ and q is _____.

14. What is the definition of Hardy-Weinberg equilibrium and what is its formula?

15. If the prevalence of the autosomal recessive disease cystic fibrosis in a population of northern Europeans is 1/2500, what is the predicted carrier status of cystic fibrosis in that population?

16. Define each of the following phrases related to population genetics.

| | Definition |
|---|---|
| **New mutation** | |
| **Natural selection** | |
| **Genetic drift** | |
| **Gene flow** | |
| **Consanguinity** | |

17. Ploidy is the number of complete sets of chromosomes in a cell. Normally, the complete set of chromosomes in humans is known as _____. _____ is the condition in which the chromosome number in a cell is not the usual number. The normal human karyotypes contain _____ autosomes and one pair of sex chromosomes with the karyotype _____ for females and _____ for males.

18. Numerical chromosome abnormalities are generally caused by _____ of sister chromatids during either meiosis 1 or meiosis 2.

19. List the disease that relates to each chromosome abnormality or state "lethal" where applicable.

| Chromosomal Abnormality | Disease |
|---|---|
| 45,X | |
| 47,XX,+21 | |
| 47,XY,+14 | |
| 47,XXY | |
| 47,XY,+18 | |
| 45,XY | |
| 47,XX,+13 | |

20. Concisely explain reciprocal translocation.

21. Concisely explain the consequence of reciprocal translocation during gametogenesis.

22. Concisely explain the consequence of reciprocal translocation in somatic cells.

23. Concisely explain Robertsonian translocation.

24. Concisely explain any pathology associated with Robertsonian translocation.

25. Microdeletions are the loss of some genetic material within a chromosome. List the disease that results from a microdeletion of the given chromosome and a hallmark of that disease.

| Chromosome | Disease | Hallmark of Disease |
|---|---|---|
| 5 | | |
| 7 | | |
| 22 | | |

## TOPIC 4: GENETIC DISEASES

1.  Fill out the following table summarizing the common genetics diseases tested on the exam.

| Name | Mode of Inheritance | Defective Gene | Pathologic Hallmark |
|------|--------------------|--------------------|---------------------|
| Achondroplasia | | | |
| Polycystic kidney disease | | | |
| Familial adenomatous polyposis | | | |
| Familial hypercholesterolemia | | | |
| Hereditary hemorrhagic telangiectasia | | | |
| Hereditary spherocytosis | | | |
| Huntington's disease | | | |
| Marfan syndrome | | | |
| Multiple endocrine neoplasia syndromes | | | |
| Neurofibromatosis 1 | | | |
| Neurofibromatosis 2 | | | |
| Tuberous sclerosis | | | |
| Von Hippel-Lindau disease | | | |
| Albinism | | | |
| Cystic fibrosis | | | |
| Phenylketonuria | | | |
| Sickle cell anemia | | | |
| Tay-Sachs disease | | | |
| Friedreich's ataxia | | | |
| Duchenne muscular dystrophy | | | |

| Name | Mode of Inheritance | Defective Gene | Pathologic Hallmark |
|---|---|---|---|
| G6PD deficiency | | | |
| Hemophilia A | | | |
| Hemophilia B | | | |
| Lesch-Nyhan syndrome | | | |
| Fragile X syndrome | | | |
| Hypophosphatemic rickets | | | |

## TOPIC 5: SIGNAL TRANSDUCTION SYSTEMS AND VITAMINS

1.  Define each of the 3 classes of hormones and provide an example.

| Hormone Classification | Definition | Example |
| --- | --- | --- |
| Autocrine | | |
| Paracrine | | |
| Endocrine | | |

2.  Why is the regulation of metabolic pathways controlled by lipid-soluble hormones much slower (hours) compared to the regulation of metabolic pathways controlled by water-soluble hormones (min)?

3.  Why do water-soluble hormones require a second messenger to control a pathway whereas lipid-soluble hormones do not?

4. The various features of signal transduction mediated by water-soluble hormones are shown below. Complete the table by filling in the empty cells.

| Pathway | G-protein | Enzyme | Second Messenger | Protein Kinase | Hormone Example |
|---|---|---|---|---|---|
| cAMP | | | cAMP | | |
| PIP2 | | Phospholipase C | | | |
| cGMP | none | | cGMP | | |
| Insulin; growth factors | | ------------------- | --------------- | | |

5. Upon hormonal stimulation of trimeric G-proteins, which subunit binds GTP to function?

6. Growth factors function through binding to their receptors on the surface of specific cells causing activation of signaling cascades in the cell leading to cellular responses. A mutation in the ras gene resulting in constitutive activation of the protein can lead to the development of cancer. Concisely explain how this process occurs.

7. Explain the biochemical relationship of glycogen synthesis in muscle and blood glucose levels in diabetics.

8.  The various features of water-soluble vitamins are shown below. Complete the table by filling in the empty cells.

| Vitamin | Coenzyme Form | One Main Function | One Hallmark of Deficiency |
|---------|---------------|-------------------|----------------------------|
| **Thiamine** (B1) | | Decarboxylation | |
| **Riboflavin** (B2) | FAD and FMN | Oxidation/reduction | |
| **Niacin** (B3) | | | |
| **Pantothenic acid** (B5) | Coenzyme A | | Rare |
| **Pyridoxine** (B6) | | Transamination | |
| **Biotin** (B7) | Biotinyl lysine | | Alopecia |
| **Folic acid** (B9) | | | Megaloblastic anemia |
| **Cobalamin** (B12) | Methylcobalamin or deoxyadenosylcobalamin | Methionine synthesis, odd-carbon fatty acid metabolism | |
| **Ascorbic acid** (C) | None; used as is | | |

9. Why do symptoms of pellagra sometimes appear after consumption of a diet consisting mostly of corn-based meals?

10. Why do deficiencies of water-soluble vitamins usually manifest with erythrocyte, skin, or neuronal problems?

11. How can megaloblastic anemia caused by vitamin $B_{12}$ be differentiated from any other vitamin deficiency?

12. Which vitamin deficiencies have cheilosis/stomatitis as a characteristic, and how are they distinguished from one another?

13. Which vitamin deficiencies have homocysteinemia as a characteristic? How are these vitamin deficiencies that have homocysteinemia distinguished from one another based on blood value information?

14. Explain the difference between dry beriberi, wet beriberi, and Wernicke-Korsakoff syndrome.

15. What is sideroblastic anemia and how is it caused?

16. The administration of which drugs can cause which water-soluble vitamins to become deficient?

17. Newborns undergoing phototherapy treatment are prone to deficiency of the water-soluble vitamin _____. Explain in biochemical terms why frequent ingestion of raw eggs might cause a person to be prone to a deficiency of one of the water-soluble vitamins.

18. The various features of the fat-soluble vitamins are shown below. Complete the table by filling in the empty cells.

| Vitamin | Active Form | One Main Function | One Hallmark of Deficiency | One Hallmark of Toxicity |
|---------|-------------|-------------------|----------------------------|--------------------------|
| **Vitamin A** | Retinol; retinoic acid<br><br>cis-Retinal | | | |
| **Vitamin D** | | Increase blood calcium | | |
| **Vitamin K** | Vitamin K as is | | | Hemolytic anemia |
| **Vitamin E** | Vitamin E as is | | | Mild bleeding when administered warfarin |

19. _____ is a highly negatively charged substance which is an anti-coagulant and functions to activate anti-thrombin III.

20. In contrast to most water-soluble vitamins, why is a true deficiency of the fat-soluble vitamins rarely seen in normal adults?

21. In the presence of warfarin, the $K_m$ of vitamin K for its enzyme would be expected to increase, decrease, or be unchanged (*circle one*).

22. What are 2 reasons why newborns are prone to vitamin K deficiency?

23. The primary event in photoreception is the light-dependent conversion of _____ bound to rhodopsin to the _____ isomer. This results in the dissociation of this isomer from rhodopsin. The consequence is a confirmation change which activates the _____ exchange activity of the $\alpha_t$ subunit of the protein called _____, which is then released, causing activation of the enzyme phosphodiesterase that cleaves _____.

# TOPIC 6: OVERVIEW OF ENERGY AND CARBOHYDRATE METABOLISM

1. The various features of the major glucose transporters are shown below. Complete the table by filling in the empty cells.

| Name | Tissues | Km Glucose | Functions |
|------|---------|-----------|-----------|
| **GLUT1** | | 1 mM | |
| **GLUT2** | | 15 mM | |
| **GLUT3** | | 1 mM | |
| **GLUT4** | | 5 mM | |

2.   Which of the following metabolites (letters A – I) correctly answers each of the statements below (1–5) concerning muscle energy metabolism?

   (A)   Phosphocreatine

   (B)   Creatinine

   (C)   ADP

   (D)   Glycogen

   (E)   Phosphoenolpyruvate

   (F)   Fructose 1,6-biphosphate

   (G)   Lactic acid

   (H)   Glucose

   (I)   Fatty acids

   1.   This material acts as an energy source during the first 3–5 seconds of strenuous activity in an anaerobic fast twitch fiber (type II). _____

   2.   This is the primary energy source for cardiac muscle. _____

   3.   This non-enzymatic reaction product is a useful indicator of kidney function. _____

   4.   This is the highest energy compound in the cell. _____

   5.   Metabolism of this energy source is linked to muscle contraction by $Ca^{2+}$ regulation. _____

3.   A transporter has a Km for glucose of 15 mM and a Vmax of 12 mM glucose/sec/mg of transporter. If the glucose concentration in peripheral blood is 5 mM, the rate of glucose transport (in mM glucose/sec/mg of transporter) will be _____.

4.  A 24-year-old student represents his college in a marathon race. Energy required for him to run this distance at the fastest speed possible would be obtained from the 5 metabolic resources listed below.

    (1)   Glycogenolysis

    (2)   Gluconeogenesis

    (3)   Creatine phosphate

    (4)   Lipolysis

    (5)   ATP stores

    Which of the following best represents the most probable sequence in which these energy stores are utilized?

    (A)   1-2-3-4-5

    (B)   4-1-3-2-5

    (C)   5-1-4-2-3

    (D)   5-2-3-1-4

    (E)   5-3-1-2-4

5.  A 25-year-old man decides to pursue a strict workout regimen with an athletic trainer. The trainer recommends several dietary supplements, including carnitine, which would help him increase his muscle mass. In which situation would carnitine be most important to skeletal muscle during exercise?

    (A)   Four attempts to bench press a 200-pound weight

    (B)   Performing 45 pushups

    (C)   Completing a 50-mile bicycle race

    (D)   Jogging on the treadmill for 15 minutes

    (E)   Running 2.5 miles

6. The oxidation of 1 mole of glucose by anaerobic glycolysis yields a net of:

    (A)  2 moles of pyruvate and 2 moles of ATP

    (B)  2 moles of pyruvate, 2 moles of NADH, and 2 moles of ATP

    (C)  2 moles of lactate and 2 moles of ATP

    (D)  2 moles of lactate, 2 moles of NADH, and 2 moles of ATP

    (E)  2 moles of lactate, 2 moles of NAD, and 2 moles of ATP

7. An Olympic runner participates in a 200-meter race. During the race, it is estimated that only 0.5 liter of oxygen will be consumed by the runner. However, more than 10 liters of oxygen would be consumed if the metabolism in this interval were entirely aerobic. The majority of ATP generated during this 200-meter race is derived from which of the following?

    (A)  Lipolysis

    (B)  Glycolysis

    (C)  Glycogenesis to glucose

    (D)  Creatine phosphate

    (E)  ATP stores

    (F)  $\beta$-oxidation of fatty acids

    (G)  Krebs cycle

    (H)  Oxidation phosphorylation

8. A genetic deficiency of glucose-6-phosphatase would be expected to produce which of the following laboratory values?

|  | Serum Glc | Serum Lactate | Serum Pyruvate |
|---|---|---|---|
| (A) | high | high | high |
| (B) | high | low | low |
| (C) | high | normal | normal |
| (D) | low | high | high |
| (E) | low | low | low |
| (F) | low | normal | normal |

9. A man presents to the emergency department after ingesting an insecticide. His respiration rate is very low. Information from the Poison Control Center indicates that this particular insecticide binds to and completely inhibits cytochrome (C) Explain concisely whether the rate of $CO_2$ production in this patient would be increased, decreased, or remain the same.

10. Explain how a person exposed to excessive amounts of CO could present with a fever.

11. A 2-year-old girl has chronic anemia, jaundice, and a moderate increase in indirect bilirubin. Her spleen is slightly enlarged and her hemoglobin level is below normal. Hemoglobin electrophoresis shows the majority is normal adult type (AA), but an abnormally high percentage is saturated with 2,3-bisphosphoglycerate. Red blood cell morphology is normal, though red cell enzyme assays reveal a severe deficiency of a single enzyme, which is likely to be _____. Explain in biochemical terms what Heinz bodies are and whether they would be likely to be seen in this patient.

12. Several oxygen dissociation curves are shown in the graph below. Assuming that curve 3 corresponds to isolated hemoglobin placed in a solution containing physiological concentrations of $CO_2$ and 2,3-bisphosphoglycerate at pH 7.0, indicate (by number) which curve reflects the following changes in conditions.

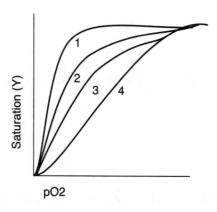

(A) Decreased $CO_2$ concentration _____

(B) Increased 2,3-bisphosphoglycerate concentration _____

(C) Increased pH _____

(D) Dissociation of hemoglobin into subunits _____

13. Under normal conditions, the rate-controlling factor in mitochondrial electron transport is the availability of _____. Under severe exercise conditions, the rate-controlling factor in mitochondrial electron transport is the availability of _____.

14. A medical student works on a farm during his summer break to earn extra money for tuition. His job is to spray tobacco plants with the chemical rotenone. He decides not to wear a mask. Consequently, he becomes sick and has convulsions, yet he recovers. Concisely explain whether the student would be expected to develop a fever during his illness.

Concisely explain whether the student would have benefited from an I.V. solution of ATP during his convulsions.

15. The various features of the major glycogen storage diseases are shown below. Complete the table by filling in the empty cells.

| Name | Deficient Enzyme | Clinical Hallmark | Glycogen Structure |
|---|---|---|---|
| von Gierke | | | Normal |
| Pompe | | | Glycogen-like material in inclusions |
| Cori | | Mild hypoglycemia Hepatomegaly | |
| Andersen | | Infantile hypotonia Cirrhosis | |
| McArdle | | | |
| Hers | | | |

16. The sensitivity of Asians (particularly those from the Pacific Rim) to alcohol has an enzymatic basis. In Asians, the ingestion of ethanol results in rapid build-up of the intoxicant acetaldehyde; compared to non-Asians, their plasma concentration of acetaldehyde rises higher and remains elevated for a longer period of time. The first 2 steps in ethanol metabolism are: ethanol → acetaldehyde → acetate (each step requiring NAD+).

   • If the Vmax values of the 2 enzymes catalyzing the reactions are the same in Asians as in non-Asians, the Km of alcohol dehydrogenase of Asians must be higher/lower/the same (*circle one*) than that of non-Asians, and the Km of acetaldehyde dehydrogenase (converts acetaldehyde to acetate) of Asians should be higher/lower/the same (*circle one*) than that of non-Asians.

   • Conversely, if the Km values of the 2 enzymes are the same in Asians as in non-Asians, the Vmax of alcohol dehydrogenase of Asians must be higher/lower/the same (*circle one*) than that of non-Asians, and the Vmax of acetaldehyde dehydrogenase of Asians should be higher/lower/ the same (*circle one*) than that of non-Asians.

# TOPIC 7: LIPID METABOLISM

1. The various features of the major lipoproteins are shown below. Complete the table by filling in the empty cells.

| Lipoprotein | Main Lipids | Main Proteins | Main Characteristics |
|---|---|---|---|
| **Chylomicrons** | TGs and cholesterol esters | | |
| **Chylomicron remnants** | | | |
| **VLDL** | | | |
| **IDL** | Cholesterol and cholesterol esters | | Intermediate particle in conversion of VLDL to LDL |
| **LDL** | | | |
| **HDL** | Relatively small amounts of cholesterol and cholesterol esters | | |

2. How is the metabolism of glucose by the hexose monophosphate shunt related to cholesterol synthesis?

3. Adipose cells manufacture triglycerides in the fed state and break triglycerides in the fasting state. In the fasting state, why are the triglycerides that are broken down not re-synthesized into triglycerides by adipose cells?

4. Insulin is released after carbohydrate intake and is involved in recruiting glucose transporters to the surface of target cells. Describe 4 ways in which insulin biochemically acts to influence lipid metabolism after glucose uptake in adipocytes and in the liver.

5. Which of the following items directly regulate the activity of acetyl-CoA carboxylase? More than one answer is possible.

   (A) Acetyl-CoA

   (B) ATP

   (C) AMP

   (D) Coenzyme A

   (E) NADH

   (F) Palmitate

   (G) Citrate

   (H) Phosphorylation by protein kinase A

   (I) All of the above

   (J) None of the above

6. Which of the following items would be found as an important component of VLDL? More than one answer is possible.

| | | | |
|---|---|---|---|
| (A) | Cholesterol | (H) | TG |
| (B) | Cholesterol ester | (I) | Free fatty acid |
| (C) | LCAT | (J) | Retinol |
| (D) | Apo A | (K) | Lipoprotein lipase |
| (E) | Apo B48 | (L) | Bile acid |
| (F) | Apo C | (M) | All of the above |
| (G) | Apo E | (N) | None of the above |

7. Defects in lipoprotein lipase predispose people to pancreatitis. If lipoprotein lipase deficiency is diagnosed early, the ill effects can be controlled.

In the presence of lipoprotein lipase deficiency, chylomicrons and VLDL levels are greatly increased in the blood. From where do these lipoprotein complexes normally come? What therapeutic strategies would be suggested for controlling chylomicron and VLDL levels? _____ Why are ascorbic acid and vitamin E particularly important with this condition?

Which of the following is true about lipoprotein lipase? More than one answer is possible.

(A) Present on the plasma membrane of adipocytes

(B) Present on the plasma membrane of endothelial cells that line adipocytes

(C) Activated by apo A

(D) Inhibited by heparin

(E) Involved in the conversion of LDL to IDL

(F) Activated by protein kinase A

(G) Synthesized by the liver

8. Concisely explain how the scavenger receptor in macrophages contributes to the process of athero-sclerosis.

9. A 17-year-old girl consults her physician because of intermittent abdominal distress. The discomfort usually follows the ingestion of a large meal, often one containing greasy or fried foods, and is accompanied by a feeling of bloating. Analysis of her stool reveals a lot of triglycerides and very little fatty acid. A diagnosis of secretion defect in pancreatic juice is made. Concisely explain whether you would support this diagnosis and/or whether there is an alternative diagnosis.

10. The various features of the major hyperlipidemias are shown below. Complete the table by filling in the empty cells.

| Type | Primary Defect | Accumulating Lipid in Blood | Accumulating Lipoprotein | Hallmarks |
|------|----------------|-----------------------------|--------------------------|-----------|
| I    |                |                             |                          |           |
| IIa  |                |                             |                          |           |
| III  |                |                             |                          | Xanthomas; atherosclerosis |
| IV   |                |                             |                          | TG-induced pancreatitis |

11. When large amounts of fatty acids are undergoing beta-oxidation in the liver in the fasting state, how is the simultaneous oxidation of glucose via glycolysis prevented?

12. A 10-year-old boy goes hiking with his father and has a prolonged episode of nausea and diarrhea after drinking unfiltered water from a stream. He is unable to eat for 2 days. They begin the long hike back to their car, but after a few miles the boy experiences extreme muscle weakness and cramping. By the time they reach the car he can no longer walk on his own. A subsequent medical exam reveals a genetic deficiency as the cause of the boy's muscle weakness. Circle the one protein that is most likely to be the problem.

(A)  Carnitine acyl transferase

(B)  Glucose-6-phosphatase

(C)  Muscle glycogen phosphorylase

(D)  Debranching enzyme

(E)  Glucose-6-phosphate dehydrogenase

(F)  Branching enzyme

(G)  Glucagon

(H)  Glucagon receptor

(I)  Hepatic glycogen phosphorylase

13. A 44-year-old alcoholic man is brought to the emergency department in a coma following a severe drinking episode. He is somewhat emaciated but has a protuberant abdomen. His urine is weakly positive for ketones by dipstick, but β-hydroxybutyrate levels in his blood and urine are very high. Blood glucose is 56 mg/dl. Biochemically explain why β-hydroxybutyrate is high in the urine but ketones are only slightly elevated.

14. Predict whether the following substances would lead to an increase, decrease, or no change in the serum level of free fatty acids if they were infused into a person.

(A) Epinephrine _____

(B) Heparin _____

(C) Prostaglandin E _____

(D) cAMP _____

(E) 10 mM glucose _____

(F) Ethanol _____

(G) Methylxanthine _____

(H) Hormone-sensitive lipase _____


15. In the first several days of starvation, the primary source of energy (ATP) to sustain muscle function is derived from the metabolic pathway _____. Under conditions of severe starvation, the primary source of energy (ATP) to sustain red blood cell function is derived from the metabolic pathway _____. Under conditions of severe starvation, the primary source of energy (ATP) to sustain liver function is derived from the specific metabolic pathway _____.


16. An unidentified 40-year-old man is brought to the emergency department in a coma. He is somewhat emaciated and has an enlarged abdomen. Laboratory tests indicate a metabolic acidosis with elevated blood lactate. His urine is weakly positive for ketones by dipstick, but β-hydroxybutyrate levels in his blood and urine are extremely high. Blood glucose is 60 mg/dL. What is the most likely diagnosis?

(A) Alcoholic coma

(B) Exercise-related hypoglycemia in a type 1 diabetic

(C) Type 2 diabetes

(D) Hypoglycemia associated with medium-chain acyl CoA dehydrogenase (MCAD) deficiency

(E) Insulin overdose

17. The various features of the major sphingolipidoses are shown below. Complete the table by filling in the empty cells.

| Name | Defective Enzyme | Accumulating Substrate | 2 Major Hallmarks |
|------|------------------|------------------------|-------------------|
| Tay-Sachs | | | |
| Gaucher's | | | |
| Niemann-Pick | | | |
| Fabry's | | Ceramide trihexoside | |
| Krabbe | | | Globoid cells<br>Peripheral neuropathy |
| Metachromatic leukodystrophy | | | Demyelination with ataxia<br>Dementia |

18. The various features of the 2 most important mucopolysaccharidoses are shown below. Complete the table by filling in the empty cells.

| Name | Defective Enzyme | Accumulating Substrate | Major Hallmark |
|------|------------------|------------------------|----------------|
| Hurler's | | | |
| Hunter's | | | |

## TOPIC 8: AMINO ACID METABOLISM

1. The diagram below shows the hepatic cycle that captures ammonia and detoxifies it. Boxes A through D represent substances or enzymes either entering or leaving the cycle. Which substance or enzyme best represents each of the boxes?

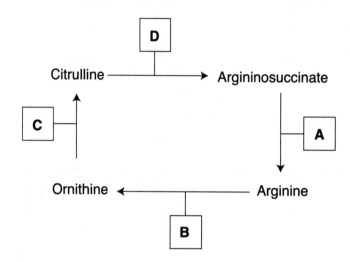

(A) _____

(B) _____

(C) _____

(D) _____

2. The definition of BUN is _____. A low BUN value would indicate that the organ _____ is malfunctioning, whereas a high BUN indicates the organ _____ is malfunctioning.

3. How is carbamoyl phosphate synthetase I deficiency distinguished from ornithine carbamoyltransferase deficiency?

4. Shown are the various features of the major genetic disorders associated with amino acids. Complete the table by filling in the empty cells.

| Name | Amino acid(s) involved | Defective Protein | Coenzyme/ cofactors needed | Clinical Hallmarks |
|---|---|---|---|---|
| **PKU** | Phe | | | |
| **Albinism** | Tyr | | copper | |
| **Alcaptonuria** | Tyr | | iron | |
| **Maple Syrup Urine Disease** | | | | |
| **Isovaleric Aciduria** | Leu | Isovaleryl CoA dehydrogenase | FAD | |
| **Cystinuria** | | | none | |
| **Hartnup Disease** | | | none | |
| **Cystathioninuria** | Met | | Pyridoxal-P | Benign |
| **Homocystinuria** | Met | | | |

5.  In catecholamine synthesis, tyrosine is converted to dopa by the enzyme
    _____, which uses _____ as a coenzyme.
    Dopa is converted by the enzyme _____ to dopamine by using the
    coenzyme _____. Dopamine is converted to norepinephrine by the
    enzyme _____, which uses _____ and
    _____ as coenzymes/cofactors. Norepinephrine is converted to
    _____ by the enzyme phenylethanolamine N-methyltransferase using
    _____ as a substrate.

6.  In the treatment of Parkinson's disease, why are carbidopa and levodopa often administered together?

7.  _____ is a tumor of the adrenal gland characterized by excessive synthesis of the catecholamines, resulting in hypertension and weight loss.

8.  Lead affects heme synthesis by affecting the enzyme _____, which is
    located in the _____ of a cell (*be specific*). The effect of lead on the
    Km of the substrate for this enzyme is increased/decreased/unchanged (*circle one*), and the effect
    of lead on the Vmax of this enzyme is increased/decreased/unchanged (*circle one*). Lead poisoning results in an accumulation of a substance that can be used diagnostically and this substance is
    _____.

9.  Briefly discuss the biochemical rationale for the most common treatment of lead poisoning.

10. The decision to fortify a widely consumed food with an essential nutrient is often politically and medically controversial. For each of the following proposed fortifications, state 1 medical reason in favor of it and 1 medical reason against.

Fortification of flour with iron:

**Pro:** _____

**Con:** _____

Fortification of flour with folate:

**Pro:** _____

**Con:** _____

11. Bacterial gut flora produce a number of reactions that have a direct bearing on human metabolism. Concisely describe the action of the flora in the following types of metabolism (state "none" if flora have no action).

a. Metabolism of a specific water-soluble vitamin

b. Metabolism of a specific fat-soluble vitamin

c. Bile acid metabolism

d. Cholesterol digestion

e. Carbohydrate digestion

f. Bilirubin metabolism

12. A 13-year-old boy playing baseball slid into home plate, sustaining a large bruise on his thigh. The bruise was initially dark red, but at the hospital where x-rays were found to be negative for fracture, the bruise turned dark blue-green. After a few days the parents bring the boy back for evaluation, concerned that the affected area is now yellow-orange. The physician reassures them and explains the events leading to the color change of the bruise in lay terms. Concisely explain the events in biochemical terms.

13. A 2-year-old girl is taken to a pediatric clinic because of persistent anemia and failure to thrive. Laboratory analysis reveals extremely low vitamin B6 levels. Would the anemia be expected to be pernicious, hemolytic, megaloblastic, or microcytic (*circle one*)? Concisely explain the biochemical relationship between the kind of anemia present and the vitamin B6 deficiency.

# TOPIC 9: PURINES AND PYRIMIDINES

1.  Several major enzymes involved in pyrimidine synthesis are shown below. List a drug that is used to inhibit the respective enzyme.

| Enzyme | Drug |
|---|---|
| Ribonucleotide reductase | |
| Thymidylate synthase | |
| Dihydrofolate reductase (in cancer cells) | |
| Dihydrofolate reductase (in microbial cells) | |
| Dihydrofolate reductase (in parasitic cells) | |

2.  Patients with gout often develop inflammation in the joints. What is the enzyme that is deficient that contributes to gout?

A deficiency in this enzyme results in the immediate buildup of which 2 compounds?
_____ Specifically, what happens when these 2 compounds build up?

What therapy is typically used for the treatment for chronic gout and why?

# PHARMACOLOGY

## TOPIC 1: PHARMACODYNAMICS AND PHARMACOKINETICS

1.  What is the equation for volume of distribution?

2.  Drugs with a low $V_d$ are found in the _____, whereas drugs with a high $V_d$ are found in _____.

3.  A new drug is found experimentally to have an apparent $V_d$ of 2000 L in a 70-kg adult. What is your interpretation of these data?

4.  Would hemodialysis be an effective way to eliminate this drug on overdose?

5.  For a drug that is not secreted or reabsorbed, how would you interpret a finding that this drug's clearance is <GFR? _____

    is >GFR? _____

6.  For a drug with a t½ (half-life) of 3 hours given by constant IV infusion, how long will it take for this drug to reach 75% of steady state?

7.  Complete the table below to compare loading dose (LD) with maintenance dose (MD).

| | LD or MD |
|---|---|
| Must know clearance to calculate | |
| Must know volume of distribution to calculate | |
| Usually administered as a single bolus | |
| Most useful in emergency situations | |
| Given to achieve steady-state plasma levels over time | |

8.  Identify the 3 drugs whose elimination represents a constant amount over time when given at high therapeutic or toxic levels.

9.  Complete the diagram below for drugs that are weak acids or weak bases.

| | |
|---|---|
| Weak Acid | R-COOH  _____<br><br>(_____) (better cleared) |
| | |
| Weak Base | _____    RNH2 +H$^+$<br><br>(better cleared) (_____) |

10. Drug #1 is a weak acid with a $pK_a$ of 4. Drug #2 is a weak base with a $pK_a$ of 8. When placed at the given pH, complete the following table.

| | pH | Mostly Ionized (I) or Nonionized (N) | Easily Crosses Membranes? Yes (Y) or No (N) |
|---|---|---|---|
| Drug #1 | 7.4 | | |
| Drug #2 | 7.4 | | |
| Drug #1 | 2 | | |
| Drug #2 | 9 | | |

11. Complete the table below using acetylation, glucuronidation, or oxidation.

| Statement | Type of Metabolism |
|---|---|
| Reduced activity in neonates | |
| Cytochrome P-450 metabolism | |
| Genotypic variation may cause SLE | |
| Metabolism of chloramphenicol | |
| Metabolism of hydralazine | |

12. P-450 inducer or inhibitor?

| | Inducer or Inhibitor |
|---|---|
| Phenytoin | |
| Erythromycin | |
| Grapefruit juice | |
| Phenobarbital | |
| Cimetidine | |
| Ritonavir | |

13. When given to a patient already receiving a full agonist, what effect will a competitive antagonist have on potency?

    Effect on efficacy?

14. When given to a patient already receiving a full agonist, what effect will a noncompetitive antagonist have on potency?

    Effect on efficacy?

15. The most dangerous drugs have a _____ TI, whereas safer drugs have a _____ TI.

# TOPIC 2: SYMPATHETIC AND PARASYMPATHETIC NERVOUS SYSTEMS

1. Complete the flowchart below for nicotinic (N) and muscarinic (M) receptor types:

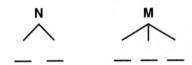

2. Identify the G-protein coupling for each receptor below using $G_s$, $G_i$, or $G_q$.

| Receptor | G-protein |
|----------|-----------|
| $M_1$ | |
| $a_1$ | |
| $D_1$ | |
| $\beta_1$ | |
| $a_2$ | |
| $b_2$ | |
| $D_2$ | |
| $M_2$ | |
| $M_3$ | |

3. Identify the drug or drug class.

| Statement | Drug |
|---|---|
| Blocks release of ACh | |
| Increases t½ of ACh | |
| Destroys adrenergic nerve terminals | |
| Promotes NE release from adrenergic nerves | |
| Stimulates negative feedback receptors on adrenergic nerves | |

4. Identify the primary use of each drug below.

| Drug | Use |
|---|---|
| Bethanechol | |
| Edrophonium | |
| Dobutamine | |
| Esmolol | |
| Pilocarpine | |
| Pyridostigmine | |
| Albuterol | |
| Tropicamide | |

5. Identify the antidote for each drug.

| Drug | Antidote |
|------|----------|
| M agonist | |
| M antagonist | |
| Irreversible AChE inhibitor | |
| β-blocker | |
| Phenylephrine | |

6. Match the drug with its action and corresponding receptor.

| Drug | Action (Agonist, Antagonist) | Receptor(s) |
|------|------------------------------|-------------|
| Prazosin | | |
| Atenolol | | |
| Methacholine | | |
| Albuterol | | |
| Epinephrine | | |
| Scopolamine | | |
| Phenoxybenzamine | | |
| Propranolol | | |
| Clonidine | | |

## TOPIC 3: TOXICOLOGY AND ADVERSE EFFECTS OF MEDICATIONS

1. Complete the table below.

| Drug or Poison | Antidote |
|---|---|
| | *N*-acetyl cysteine |
| Aspirin | |
| Iron | |
| | Methylene blue |
| Opioids | |
| | Fomepizole |
| Heparin | |
| Warfarin (rapid reversal) | |
| | Flumazenil |

2. Complete the table below for the alcohols and their metabolism.

| Alcohol | Aldehyde | Acid |
|---|---|---|
| Ethanol | | |
| Ethylene glycol | | |
| Methanol | | |

3. Match the alcohol with its side effect.

| Alcohol | Side Effect |
| --- | --- |
|  | Ocular damage |
|  | Nephrotoxicity |
|  | Nausea, vomiting, headache |

4. What enzyme is inhibited by the drug disulfiram?

5. What substance accumulates as a result of drinking alcohol at the same time disulfiram is used?

# IMMUNOLOGY, HEMATOLOGY, AND ONCOLOGY

## TOPIC 1: BLOOD CELLS AND LYMPHOID STRUCTURES

1.  Fill in the table below for each of the white blood cells.

| Cell Type | Identification (CD Marker and/or Description) | | Function | |
|---|---|---|---|---|
| Neutrophil | | | | |
| Monocyte | | | | |
| Macrophage | | | | |
| Eosinophils | | | | |
| Basophil | | | | |
| Mast cell | | | | |
| Dendritic cell | | | | |
| Lymphocytes | **B cells** | **T cells** | **B cells** | **T cells** |
| | | | | |
| Plasma cells | | | | |

2. Fill in the table below for each description of the lymph node anatomy.

| Description | Lymph Node Structure |
|---|---|
| Plasma cells and memory region | |
| T cell-rich region | |
| B cell-rich region | |
| B cell activation occurs here | |
| Antigens enter the lymph node | |
| Activated and memory cells leave the lymph node | |

3. Name the site where naïve B cells and T cells enter the lymph nodes.

4. Name the T cell-rich region of the spleen.

5. Name the B cell-rich region of the spleen.

6. A patient with asplenia would have an increased risk of infection from which types of organisms?

7. List 3 signs of asplenia.

8.  For each description below, list a "C" if it occurs or is found in the thymic cortex or an "M" if it occurs or is found in the thymic medulla.

| Description | Region of Thymus |
|---|---|
| Immature T cells are found here | |
| Mature T cells are found here | |
| T cell selection occurs here | |

9.  For the different stages of T cell development, place a "+," if the stage has a marker listed and a "–" if it does not.

| Stage of Development | CD3 | CD4 | CD8 | T Cell Receptor |
|---|---|---|---|---|
| Pre-thymic (pro-T cells) | | | | |
| Immature T cells found in the cortex | | | | |
| Mature T$_H$ cells | | | | |
| Mature T$_C$ cells | | | | |

# TOPIC 2: T CELL AND B CELL FUNCTION

1. Fill in the following table regarding MHC.

| Description | MHC Class I | MHC Class II |
|---|---|---|
| Tissue distribution | | |
| Recognized by | | |
| Type of peptides bound within | | |
| Where is antigen loaded? | | |

2. For each disease below, list the associated HLA type. Some diseases may be associated with more than one HLA type.

| Disease | Associated HLA Type |
|---|---|
| Systemic lupus erythematosus | |
| Goodpasture's disease | |
| Ankylosing spondylitis | |
| Type 1 diabetes | |
| Multiple sclerosis | |
| Rheumatoid arthritis | |
| Hashimoto's thyroiditis | |
| Graves' disease | |
| Reactive arthritis | |

3. Name the function of NK cells.

4. Describe 2 mechanisms for NK cell killing.

5. List the cytokine that is important for differentiation from a Th0 to a Th1 cell. From a Th0 to a Th2 cell?

6. Describe the function of the Th1 cells?

   Of the Th2 cells?

7. List signal 1 for CTL activation. _____

   List signal 2 for CTL activation. _____

8. List signal 1 for plasma cell activation. _____

   List signal 2 for plasma cell activation. _____

9. Which Th1 cytokine inhibits Th2 cell development? _____

10. Which Th2 cytokine(s) inhibits Th1 cell development? _____

11. List the 5 heavy chain classes of antibodies. _____

12. What is the function of the Fc region of the antibody molecule?


    Of the Fab region?


13. List 3 functions of antibodies.


14. Fill in the following table with a "+" if the antibody has that function or "–" if the antibody does not have that function.

| Function | IgM | IgD | IgG | IgA | IgE |
|---|---|---|---|---|---|
| Complements activation | | | | | |
| Opsonization | | | | | |
| Antibody dependent cellular cytotoxicity (ADCC) | | | | | |
| Crosses the placenta | | | | | |
| Triggers mast cell granule release | | | | | |
| Predominates in the primary immune response | | | | | |
| Predominates in the secondary immune response | | | | | |

15. LPS is an example of a _____ antigen that can produce only

    _____ (Ab class).

16. For each cytokine below, list the cell type that makes it and its major function. Note that while many cytokines have multiple roles, only the major function should be listed here.

| Cytokine | Made by (Cell) | Major Function |
|----------|----------------|----------------|
| IL-1 | | |
| IL-2 | | |
| IL-4 | | |
| IL-5 | | |
| IL-6 | | |
| IL-8 | | |
| IL-10 | | |
| IFN-$\gamma$ | | |
| TNF-$\alpha$ | | |

17. For each CD marker listed, write the cell type on which it is expressed.

| CD Marker | Cell Type |
|-----------|-----------|
| CD19 | |
| CD3 | |
| CD56 | |
| CD21 | |
| CD16 | |
| CD14 | |
| CD28 | |

Immunology, Hematology, and Oncology

18. Using the diagram below, draw where superantigens interact with the TCR and class II MHC.

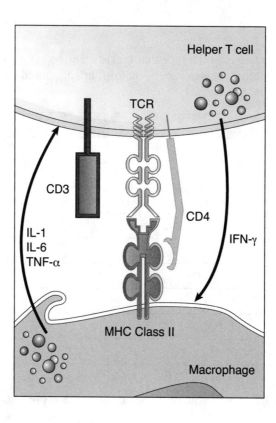

19. For each example given, list whether it is an example of natural passive immunity "NP," natural active immunity "NA," artificial active immunity "AA" or artificial passive immunity "AP."

| Example | Type of Immunity |
| --- | --- |
| Placental IgG | |
| Recovery from primary varicella zoster | |
| Anti-rabies immune globulin | |
| MMR vaccine | |
| Anti-venin after a snake bite | |

## TOPIC 3: IMMUNE HYPERSENSITIVITY

1. The cytokines essential in the development of toxic shock syndrome from activation of superantigens are:

2. The CD marker that binds to LPS is _____.

3. Define antigenic variation.

4. For each agent listed, write the antigen that undergoes antigenic variation.

   *Salmonella:* _____

   *Neisseria gonorhoeae:* _____

   Influenza: _____

5. Order the following events that occur in a type I hypersensitivity reaction by placing numbers 1 through 7 on the lines provided.

   _____ Allergen cross-links several IgE molecules on mast cells

   _____ B cells produce IgE

   _____ Exposure to allergen

   _____ Degranulation

   _____ IgE binds to mast cells via FcR

   _____ $T_H2$ mediated class switch to IgE

   _____ Re-exposure to allergen

Immunology, Hematology, and Oncology

6. Describe the mechanism of tissue destruction in a cytotoxic type II hypersensitivity reaction.

7. Describe the mechanism of tissue destruction in a type III hypersensitivity reaction.

8. What is the name for a localized type III reaction?

9. Describe the mechanism of a type IV hypersensitivity reaction.

10. List the first antibody produced in response to an allergen.

11. For each disease below, list the type of hypersensitivity reaction (type I, II, III, or IV).

| Disease | Hypersensitivity Reaction |
|---|---|
| Post-streptococcal glomerulonephritis | |
| Systemic lupus erythematosus | |
| Allergic rhinitis | |
| Hemolytic disease of the newborn | |
| Transfusion reactions | |
| Hashimoto's thyroiditis | |
| Serum sickness | |
| Hay fever | |
| Rheumatic fever | |
| Multiple sclerosis | |
| PPD skin test | |

Immunology, Hematology, and Oncology

12. For the autoimmune diseases listed, write in the autoantigen(s) associated with each disease.

| Autoimmune Disease | Autoantigen(s) |
|---|---|
| Graves' disease | |
| Systemic lupus erythematosus | |
| Rheumatoid arthritis | |
| Scleroderma | |
| Celiac disease | |
| Goodpasture's disease | |
| Pemphigus | |
| Hashimoto's thyroiditis | |
| Type 1 diabetes | |
| Sjögren's disease | |
| Wegener's granulomatosis | |
| Churg-Strauss syndrome | |

# TOPIC 4: IMMUNODEFICIENCY AND ORGAN TRANSPLANT

1. For the listed symptoms or lab values, fill in the corresponding immunodeficiency disease and if the disease is X-linked.

| Symptoms | Immunodeficiency Disease | X-linked |
|---|---|---|
| ↑ IgM, ↓ IgG, IgA, and IgE | | |
| Recurrent GI and respiratory infections | | |
| No peripheral B cells, no Igs, recurrent bacterial infections | | |
| Hypogammaglobulinemia that begins in late teens/early 20s | | |

2. List the major types of infections to which DiGeorge's syndrome patients are susceptible.

3. List the major types of infections to which patients with IL-12 receptor deficiency are susceptible.

4. The cytokine that is deficient in Job syndrome is called _____.

5. List 3 causes of severe combined immunodeficiency disease (SCID).

6. List the triad of symptoms observed in Wiskott-Aldrich syndrome.

7. For each phagocytic immunodeficiency listed, name the mutation and the symptoms associated with each.

| Disease | Mutation | Symptoms |
|---|---|---|
| Chronic granulomatous disease | | |
| Leukocyte adhesion deficiency | | |
| Chédiak-Higashi syndrome | | |

8. Define the following terms:

- Autograft

- Isograft

- Allograft

- Xenograft

9. List the types of graft rejection from the fastest rejection to the slowest rejection.

10. Define graft-versus-host disease.

11. Major side effects for cyclosporine and tacrolimus drugs include _____.

12. Name the mechanism of action of sirolimus.


13. Complete the diagram below.

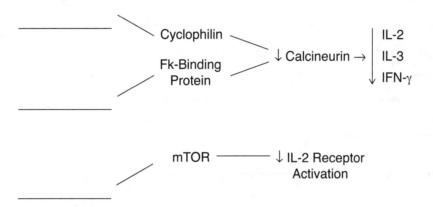

14. For each biologic agent listed, write the mechanism of action.

| Monoclonal Antibody | MOA |
| --- | --- |
| Daclizumab | |
| Muromonab | |

15. For each recombinant cytokine listed in the table, list the major clinical uses.

| Recombinant Cytokine | Clinical Uses |
| --- | --- |
| Aldesleukin | |
| Erythropoietin | |
| IFN-α | |
| IFN-β | |
| IFN-γ | |
| IL-11 | |

16. For each biologic drug listed, write in the mechanism of action.

| Biologic | Mechanism of Action |
|---|---|
| Infliximab | |
| Adalimumab | |
| Abciximab | |
| Trastuzumab | |
| Rituximab | |

17. Match the antibody drug with its target.

| Drug | Target |
|---|---|
| Trastuzumab | |
| | IL-2 receptors |
| Abciximab | |
| | TNF-$\alpha$ |

## TOPIC 5: LYMPHOMA AND MULTIPLE MYELOMA

1.  Would a patient with increased leukocytes and a left shift in peripheral blood most likely have a low, normal, or elevated leukocyte alkaline phosphatase?

2.  Is Epstein-Barr virus more likely to be associated with Hodgkin's lymphoma or non-Hodgkin's lymphoma (NHL)? Which type of lymphoma is associated with HIV?

3.  Is Hodgkin's lymphoma or NHL more likely to produce constitutional symptoms such as weight loss, fatigue, and night sweats?

4.  What immunohistochemical staining pattern is typical for a Reed-Sternberg cell?

5.  A lymph node biopsy showing areas of fibrosis with the intervening tissue containing a mixture of lymphocytes, histiocytes, scattered eosinophils, plasma cells, and lacunar-type Reed-Sternberg cells is most likely what type of lymphoma?

6.  What characterizes stage 3 Hodgkin's lymphoma?

7. Complete the following table.

| Disease | Translocation |
| --- | --- |
| Burkitt's lymphoma | |
| Mantle cell lymphoma | |
| Follicular lymphoma | |

8. Adult T cell leukemia is associated with _____ virus.

9. Cells with unusual cerebriform nuclei found in peripheral blood are most likely to be of what leukocyte lineage?

10. Multiple "punched out" lesions in the ribs and spine on x-ray studies suggest what hematologic malignancy?

11. What type of immunoglobulin chains tend to accumulate in kidney tubules of myeloma patients?

12. Would calcium levels be increased or decreased in multiple myeloma?

13. Would rouleaux formation in the peripheral blood be more likely to suggest Hodgkin's disease, multiple myeloma, or follicular lymphoma?

14. What is the most likely diagnosis of a 65-year-old man who presents with priapism, is found to have an M-protein spike on serum protein electrophoresis, but does not have lytic lesions on x-ray?

15. What is the most likely diagnosis in a 62-year-old asymptomatic woman with an M-protein spike on serum electrophoresis?

Immunology, Hematology, and Oncology

## TOPIC 6: LEUKEMIA AND MYELOPROLIFERATIVE DISORDERS

1.  What is suggested by positive CD10 in a leukemic patient?

2.  Would warm autoimmune hemolytic anemia be more likely to be seen in acute lymphocytic leukemia, chronic lymphocytic leukemia, acute myelogenous leukemia, or chronic myelogenous leukemia?

3.  A patient whose lymphocytes have long, wavy projections in the peripheral blood might now be potentially cured with which drug that acts as an enzyme inhibitor?

4.  What enzyme can be helpful in the diagnosis of hairy cell leukemia?

5.  What translocation is associated with most types of acute myelogenous leukemia? With acute promyelocytic leukemia?

6.  What can be used to treat the M3 (acute promyelocytic leukemia) subtype of AML?

7.  Chronic myelogenous leukemia can be specifically targeted by which drug that targets the product of the translocation?

8. Treatment of the M3 subtype of AML can cause what complication?

9. Complete the table below.

| Disease | Translocation | Gene/Product Association | Cause of Disease |
|---------|---------------|--------------------------|------------------|
| CML | | | |
| Burkitt's lymphoma | | | |
| Follicular lymphoma | | | |
| AML-M3 | | | |
| Ewing's sarcoma | | | |
| Mantle cell lymphoma | | | |

10. Electron microscopy of a tumor shows tennis racquet-shaped cytoplasmic organelles. This is most likely a tumor of what cells?

11. What are 2 markers of Langerhans cell histiocytosis?

12. What 2 chronic myeloproliferative disorders are likely to evolve into myelofibrosis? What 2 are likely to evolve into acute leukemia?

Immunology, Hematology, and Oncology

13. Teardrop cells in the peripheral blood suggest which myeloproliferative disorder?

14. In polycythemia vera, are erythropoietin levels usually decreased or increased?

15. Which 3 myeloproliferative disorders are associated with the JAK2 mutation?

16. What is the term used when the liver and spleen produce red cells?

17. Polycythemia vera can be associated with which diseases?

18. For each pathogen below, list the type(s) of associated cancer. As some agents may cause multiple types of cancer, list them all.

| Pathogen | Cancer |
|---|---|
| HTLV | |
| HBV/HCV | |
| EBV | |
| HPV | |
| HHV-8 | |
| HIV | |
| *Helicobacter pylori* | |
| *Schistosoma haematobium* | |

## TOPIC 7: DNA REPLICATION AND REPAIR

1.  In heterochromatin, genes are inactive due to _____. In euchromatin, genes are active due to _____.

2.  Circle the histone that is not in a nucleosome: H1, H2A, H2B, H3, H4.

3.  In the liver, where is the gene for factor VIII specifically located?

    Circle one: euchromatin, heterochromatin, not present

    In the liver, where is the gene for β-globin specifically located?

    Circle one: euchromatin, heterochromatin, not present

    In the erythrocyte, where is the gene for β-globin specifically located?

    Circle one: euchromatin, heterochromatin, not present

4.  The key regulated enzyme of purine synthesis is _____ and it is allosterically inhibited by the purine nucleotides _____, _____, and _____. Pharmacologically, the enzyme is a target of the antineoplastic drug _____. Why can this pharmacologic drug be used for the treatment of cancerous cells and yet not affect normal human cells?

5.  Carbamoyl phosphate synthetase II is located _____ of most cells and uses _____, _____, and _____ as substrates to synthesize carbamoyl phosphate.

6. What are the 2 reactions catalyzed by UMP synthase?

7. Why does a deficiency of ornithine transcarbamylase in the urea cycle result in orotic aciduria?

8. The enzyme that converts UMP to dUMP is _____, which can be inhibited by the drug _____. The enzyme that converts dUMP to dTMP is _____, which can be inhibited by the drug _____.

9. Dihydrofolate reductase converts _____ to _____ and uses _____ as coenzyme. This enzyme in eukaryotes can be inhibited by the anticancer drug _____ and in prokaryotes by _____ or _____.

# TOPIC 8: ANTINEOPLASTIC AND ANTIMETABOLITE DRUGS

1.  For each antineoplastic drug, identify if it is cell-cycle specific (CCS) or non-cell cycle specific (NCSS). For each CCS drug, identify in which phase of the cell cycle the drug works.

| Drug | CCS or NCSS | Cell Cycle Phase |
|---|---|---|
| Methotrexate | | |
| Doxorubicin | | |
| Vincristine | | |
| Cyclophosphamide | | |
| Cisplatin | | |
| 6-Mercaptopurine | | |
| Bleomycin | | |
| Etoposide | | |

2.  Match the toxicity with the antineoplastic drug that may cause it.

| Drug | Toxicity |
|---|---|
| | Peripheral neuropathy |
| | Dilated cardiomyopathy |
| | Pulmonary fibrosis |
| | Nephrotoxicity |
| | Hemorrhagic cystitis |

Immunology, Hematology, and Oncology

3.  Match the cancer drug with its cellular target.

| Drug | Target |
| --- | --- |
| Paclitaxel | |
| Methotrexate | |
| 5-Fluorouracil | |
| Etoposide | |
| Cyclophosphamide | |
| Hydroxyurea | |
| Tamoxifen | |

# TOPIC 9: NONHEMOLYTIC ANEMIA AND PORPHYRIA

1.  What transporter on the RBC excretes excess bicarbonate that accumulates in the RBC?

2.  What is the average life span of a red blood cell?

3.  In an individual with type B blood, erythrocytes would have which antigens? What antibodies could be present in the serum?

4.  What blood type is the universal donor? Universal recipient?

5.  What is given to Rh– mothers prior to delivery to prevent formation of anti-Rh+ antibodies?

6.  Describe the structure of heme in basic terms.

7.  What action does heme have on ALA synthase?

8.  What enzymes are inhibited by lead poisoning?

9.  Complete the mnemonic below for key facts about lead poisoning.

L

E

**A**
**D** ⟩ Enzyme inhibited by lead is: _____

**P**
**A** ⟩ Common symptom in heavy metal poisoning: _____

I

**N** – Symptom of lead poisoning: _____

T

**E** – Symptom of lead poisoning: _____

**A** – Characteristic hematologic finding: _____

**T** – Treat with: _____

**E** – _____

R

**S** – _____

10. What enzyme is deficient in acute intermittent porphyria?

11. How does acute intermittent porphyria present?

12. What enzyme is deficient in porphyria cutanea tarda?

13. What are the skin manifestations of porphyria cutanea tarda?

14. An anemia in which the mean corpuscular volume of the erythrocytes is 115 fL would be considered microcytic, normocytic, or macrocytic?

15. Would a peripheral smear that showed small, pale erythrocytes most likely be due to folate deficiency, iron deficiency, or vitamin B12 deficiency?

16. Hemoglobin H disease is caused by what genetic composition?

17. What is the result of deletion of 4 α chain genes?

18. An asymptomatic patient suspected of having β-thalassemia minor should be tested for what form of hemoglobin?

19. An X-linked defect in ALA synthase can cause what type of anemia?

20. Microcytic anemia due to lead poisoning can be treated with which drugs?

21. Macrocytic anemia related to vitamin B12 deficiency would most likely be caused by which diseases?

22. How can folate deficiency be distinguished from B12 deficiency?

23. What processes can cause non-megaloblastic anemia?

## TOPIC 10: HEMOLYTIC ANEMIA AND PATHOLOGIC RED BLOOD CELL FORMS

1. What is the difference between intravascular and intrinsic hemolysis? Between extravascular and extrinsic hemolysis?

2. Would a patient with low haptoglobin, high LDH, and hemoglobinuria be most likely to have intravascular hemolysis or extravascular hemolysis?

3. Ankyrin and spectrin may be defective in which hemolytic anemia?

4. Upon entry into a cell, glucose is phosphorylated to become glucose 6-phosphate. List the 3 separate metabolic pathways it can then enter and the purpose of each pathway.

   a.

   b.

   c.

5. In glycolysis, the oxidation of glyceraldehyde 3-phosphate to 1,3-bisphosphoglycerate results in the conversion of NAD to NADH. The function of the NADH is to

   _____.

Immunology, Hematology, and Oncology

6.  In the hexose monophosphate shunt, the oxidation of glucose 6-phosphate by the enzyme G6PD results in the conversion of NADP to NADPH. In erythrocytes, what is the function of NADPH?

7.  In which hemolytic anemia are Howell-Jolly bodies and osmotic fragility typical and erythrocytes more susceptible to oxidative stress secondary to low levels of glutathione?

8.  What is the mode of inheritance of G6PD deficiency?

9.  What are some precipitating factors for hemolysis in G6PD deficiency?

10. What is a Heinz body and how is it formed?

11. Why are certain drugs such as sulfa drugs not administered to an individual with G6PD deficiency?

12. Why is an individual with G6PD deficiency expected to have hemolytic anemia?

13. What glycolytic enzyme deficiency can often lead to hemolytic anemia?

14. Why is an individual with pyruvate kinase deficiency expected to have hemolytic anemia?

15. How is hemolytic anemia caused by G6PD deficiency distinguished from pyruvate kinase deficiency?

16. What is the cause of sickle cell anemia?

17. Which virus causes aplastic crises in sickle cell patients?

18. What renal complication is characteristically associated with sickle cell anemia?

19. What can be used in sickle cell disease to increase HbF?

20. What is the biochemical defect in HbC disease?

21. Which CD marker is characteristically negative in paroxysmal nocturnal hemoglobinuria?

22. Abnormality of which RBC membrane protein causes paroxysmal nocturnal hemoglobinuria?

Immunology, Hematology, and Oncology

23. In both the innate response and the adaptive response, formation of which complement factor leads to C5 production (that in turn leads to formation of the membrane attack complex)?

24. C1 esterase inhibitor deficiency produces which disease? _____

25. Which of the complement deficiencies are most strongly associated with anaphylactic shock?

26. Is warm agglutinin autoimmune hemolytic anemia mediated by IgM or IgG antibodies? Cold agglutinin hemolytic anemia?

27. What is an autoimmune hemolytic anemia that develops when an Rh-negative mother creates antibodies against an Rh-positive fetus?

28. What does the direct Coombs test look for?

    Indirect Coombs test?

29. Damage to RBCs during passage through narrowed vessels can produce what altered RBC form?

30. What disease is suggested by a Maltese cross appearance in erythrocytes in a peripheral smear?

31. Acanthocytes are found in what disease?

32. Basophilic stippling is seen in which diseases?

33. Bite cells are seen in what disease?

34. The mechanism underlying elliptocytosis is similar to the process underlying what other erythrocyte pathology?

35. Fragmented red blood cells are seen in which diseases?

36. Damage to a red cell by an artificial heart valve would produce what altered erythrocyte form?

37. Teardrop cells typically signal the presence of what process?

38. Target cells are found in which diseases?

39. Fill in the following table.

| Disease | Serum Iron | Transferrin (TIBC) | Ferritin |
|---|---|---|---|
| Iron deficiency | | | |
| Anemia of chronic disease | | | |
| Hemochromatosis | | | |

# TOPIC 11: THE NORMAL COAGULATION CASCADE AND PLATELET PLUG

1.  What initiates the extrinsic coagulation pathway? Intrinsic coagulation pathway?

2.  Fill in the following table about the kinin cascade.

| Molecule | Function |
|---|---|
| HMWK | |
| Factor XIIa | |
| Kallikrein | |
| Bradykinin | |
| Plasmin | |
| ACE | |

3.  Which cofactors related to the clotting cascade require vitamin K for synthesis?

4.  Warfarin inhibits what step in vitamin K-dependent synthesis of clotting factors?

5.  After initiating therapy with warfarin, what clotting factor is the first one affected? Why?

6. The mutation causing factor V Leiden does what?

7. What is the pathway of platelet production starting with a hematopoietic stem cell?

8. What do the platelet dense bodies contain?

9. Match the drug with its target.

| Drug | Target |
|------|--------|
| Aspirin | |
| Clopidogrel | |
| Warfarin | |
| Heparin | |
| Lepirudin | |

10. Fill in the following table.

| Disease | Cause of Defective Platelet Formation |
|---------|---------------------------------------|
| Bernard-Soulier syndrome | |
| Glanzmann thrombasthenia | |
| Von Willebrand disease | |

## TOPIC 12: COAGULATION AND PLATELET DISORDERS

1.  Which factors are indirectly tested in the prothrombin time? Partial thromboplastin time?

2.  Name 3 conditions that can cause a failure to clot related to low factor levels.

3.  What effect on the PT and PTT do Bernard-Soulier syndrome and Glanzmann thrombasthenia have?

4.  What constitutes the characteristic pentad of TTP?

5.  How does hemolytic-uremic syndrome (HUS) present differently from TTP?

6.  What differences in the peripheral smear are seen between idiopathic thrombocytopenic purpura (ITP) and thrombotic thrombocytopenic purpura (TTP)?

7.  Why does the PTT increase in von Willebrand disease?

8.  What features are useful in diagnosis of disseminated intravascular coagulation?

9.  Fill in the following table.

| Condition | Causes of Excessive Thrombosis |
|---|---|
| Protein C or S | |
| Factor V Leiden | |
| Prothrombin gene mutation | |
| ATIII deficiency | |

10. In each clinical scenario below, identify the drug most likely to be used.

| Scenario | Drug |
|---|---|
| Stable patient with PE | |
| Emergency management of stroke | |
| Prophylaxis for TIAs | |
| Alternative to aspirin post-MI | |
| Pregnant patient needing anticoagulant | |
| Patient with HIT needing anticoagulant | |
| Excessive bleeding following use of alteplase | |
| Rapid reversal of heparin | |

# INFECTIOUS DISEASE

## TOPIC 1: INTRODUCTION TO BACTERIOLOGY

1.  For each of the following bacterial properties listed, fill in G+ if it is found only in Gram-positive bacteria, G– if it is found only in Gram-negative bacteria, or BOTH if it is found in BOTH.

| Bacterial Property | G+, G–, or Both |
| --- | --- |
| Outer membrane | |
| LPS | |
| Thick peptidoglycan layer | |
| Thin peptidoglycan layer | |
| Cytoplasmic membrane | |
| Teichoic acid | |
| Stains pink in Gram stain | |
| Stains purple in Gram stain | |

2.  List the 4 types of antibiotics that target the cell wall:

    _____

    _____

    _____

    _____

3. Which bacterial genera have mycolic acid in the cell wall?

4. Antibiotics would work best at which stage of the bacterial growth curve?

5. A flask is inoculated to a density of $5 \times 10^3$ cells/ml. What is the density of cells in the culture after 70 minutes if the generation time is 20 minutes and the lag time is 10 minutes?

6. Place an "X" under the genetic mechanism (transformation, transduction, etc) that utilizes or would be affected by the given requirement. Some rows may have multiple Xs.

| Requirement | Hfr | Transduction | Conjugation | Transformation |
|---|---|---|---|---|
| Requires phage | | | | |
| Majority of multi-drug resistant organisms arise from this | | | | |
| Homologous recombination is required | | | | |
| Naked DNA is required | | | | |
| Cell-to-cell contact is required | | | | |
| oriT is required for transfer of genetic information | | | | |
| OriT + *tra* is required for transfer | | | | |

7. Define specialized transduction.

8. List the virulence factors acquired via specialized transduction.

9. Lipopolysaccharide (LPS) is also called _____; the toxic portion of the LPS is the

_____.

10. Exotoxins are _____ from bacterial cells. Many of these toxins are A-B toxins
    in which the A portion is the _____ portion of the toxin and the B portion is the

    _____.

11. For each bacterial toxin listed, put an "X" in the column that reflects its mechanism of action.

| Toxin | cAMP Inducer | Inhibition of Protein Synthesis |
|---|---|---|
| Anthrax | | |
| Diphtheria | | |
| Cholera | | |
| Shiga (Shiga-like) | | |
| Pertussis | | |
| ETEC | | |
| *Pseudomonas* exotoxin | | |

## TOPIC 2: INFECTIOUS DISEASES

1. Fill in the following table with the appropriate culture medium for the organisms listed.

| Organism | Culture Media |
|---|---|
| *Haemophilus influenzae* | |
| Gram-negative enteric | |
| Fungi | |
| *Neisseria gonorrhoeae* | |
| *Legionella pneumophila* | |

2. For each case description below, list the top 3 bacterial causative agents.

A 68-year-old male presents with a fever, shaking chills, and difficulty breathing. A right-sided lobar consolidation was noted on x-ray.

A 50-year-old male presents with a dry cough, headache, and low-grade fever. An interstitial pattern is noted on x-ray.

3. The treatment for streptococcal pharyngitis is _____.

4. The treatment for pharyngitis caused by *Corynebacterium diphtheriae* is

_____.

5. For each case description below, list the top 2 bacterial causative agents.

   A 4-year-old unvaccinated male develops difficulty swallowing, stridor, and drooling.

   A 28-year-old female develops sinus pressure and a purulent nasal discharge.

6. For each symptom or organism listed in the table below, place an "X" in the column that reflects whether it occurs during otitis media, otitis externa, or both.

| Disease | Fever | Ear Pain | Bulging Tympanic Membrane | *Pseudomonas aeruginosa* | *Streptococcus pneumoniae or Haemophilus influenzae* | "Swimmer's Ear" |
|---|---|---|---|---|---|---|
| Otitis externa | | | | | | |
| Otitis media | | | | | | |

7. For each organism that causes gastroenteritis, place an "I" for invasive (generally bloody diarrhea), a "T" for toxin mediated (generally watery diarrhea), or a "B" for both.

| Organism | Pathogenesis |
|---|---|
| *Campylobacter jejuni* | |
| *Salmonella* | |
| *Shigella* | |
| *Bacillus cereus* | |
| *Clostridium botulinum* | |
| *Vibrio cholerae* | |
| EHEC | |

8.  What is the most common cause of both community-acquired and nosocomial urinary tract infection?

9.  A patient who develops kidney stones likely has a urinary tract infection with _____, which produces _____, which in turn raises the urine pH to cause the formation of the stones.

10. Name the most common causative agent of osteomyelitis.

11. List the most common causative agent of septic arthritis that affects a single joint.

12. For the following evaluation of bacterial versus viral meningitis, put a ↑ if the lab values are increased, ↓ if the lab values are decreased, or N if the lab values stay normal.

| CSF Findings | Bacterial Meningitis | Viral Meningitis |
|---|---|---|
| Glucose | | |
| Lymphocytes | | |
| PMNs | | |
| Protein | | |

13. List the top 3 causes of neonatal meningitis.

14. A college student presents with bacterial meningitis. What is the most likely cause? Is there a vaccine available?

15. For each organism associated with genital infections, indicate whether each presents with a discharge or lesion.

| Organism | Discharge | Lesion |
|---|---|---|
| Neisseria gonorrhoeae | | |
| Chlamydia trachomatis (D-K) | | |
| Treponema pallidum | | |
| Bacterial vaginosis | | |
| Trichomonas vaginalis | | |
| Herpes simplex virus | | |

16. Describe the discharge or lesion, as you indicated in the question above.

| Organism | Discharge | Lesion |
|---|---|---|
| Neisseria gonorrhoeae | | |
| Chlamydia trachomatis (D-K) | | |
| Treponema pallidum | | |
| Bacterial vaginosis | | |
| Trichomonas vaginalis | | |
| Herpes simplex virus | | |

## TOPIC 3: GRAM-POSITIVES

1.  Complete the flow chart below for the Gram-positive bacteria. Genus designation is sufficient.

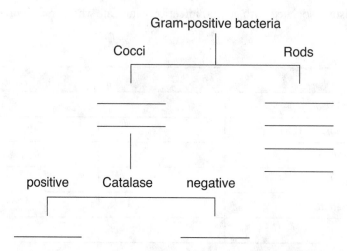

2.  For the Gram-positive cocci listed below, place an α, β, or γ for the hemolytic pattern on blood agar.

| Organism | Hemolytic Pattern on Blood Agar |
|---|---|
| *Staphylococcus aureus* | |
| *Staphylococcus epidermidis* | |
| *Staphylococcus saprophyticus* | |
| *Streptococcus pyogenes* | |
| *Streptococcus agalactiae* | |
| *Streptococcus pneumoniae* | |
| *Streptococcus mutans* | |
| *Streptococcus bovis* | |

3. List at least 5 genera or families that can cause infections in patients with chronic granulomatous disease.

   What property do the above organisms have in common?

4. Protein A is made by _____ and functions by binding to the _____ portion of the antibody to prevent _____.

5. Identify the appropriate virulence factors for the staphylococcal diseases listed below.

| Staphylococcal Diseases | |
|---|---|
| Gastroenteritis | |
| Toxic shock syndrome | |

6. A 58-year-old woman with an artificial heart valve would most likely get _____ from *Staphylococcus* _____.

7. Fill in the appropriate type of hemolysis with the descriptions below.

| Description | Hemolytic Pattern |
|---|---|
| Partial | |
| Complete | |
| No hemolysis | |

Infectious Disease

8. List the 3 diseases for which *Streptococcus pneumoniae* is the most common cause.

9. Name the bacterial group that is associated with dental caries and endocarditis due to damaged heart valves.

10. Name the major virulence factor for *Streptococcus pyogenes* that is anti-phagocytic?

11. What are 2 important features of *Listeria monocytogenes*?

12. Name the bacterium with a polypeptide instead of a polysaccharide capsule.

13. Check off the Clostridium species that produce the described toxins. Some descriptions may be found in multiple organisms.

| Toxin | (C) botulinum | (C) tetani | (C) perfringens | (C) difficile |
|---|---|---|---|---|
| Inhibits GABA, glycine | | | | |
| Inhibits release of acetylcholine | | | | |
| A-B toxin | | | | |
| α toxin | | | | |
| Enterotoxin | | | | |

Infectious Disease

14. Identify whether the following descriptions are characteristic of *Nocardia* or *Actinomyces*. Some descriptions may apply to both organisms.

| Description | Nocardia | Actinomyces |
|---|---|---|
| Endogenous infection | | |
| Exogenous infection | | |
| Aerobic | | |
| Anaerobic | | |
| Partially acid fast | | |
| Gram-positive branching rods | | |
| Infections in immune-compromised patients | | |

Infectious Disease

## TOPIC 4: GRAM-NEGATIVES

1. Fill in the table with an "M" for *Neisseria meningitidis*, a "G" for *Neisseria gonorrhoeae,* or a "B" for both.

| Description | Causative Agent |
| --- | --- |
| Capsule | |
| Ferments maltose | |
| Ferments glucose | |
| Grows on chocolate agar | |
| Growth selected on Thayer-Martin agar | |
| Commonly produces β-lactamases | |
| Oxidase positive | |
| Vaccine available | |
| Antigenic variation | |

2. *Haemophilus influenzae* in grown on _____ agar because it requires _____ and _____ factors.

3. List 3 diseases caused by *Haemophilus influenzae*.

4. Fill in the flow chart with the following bacterial genera: *Escherichia, Klebsiella, Salmonella, Shigella, Yersinia,* and *Proteus.*

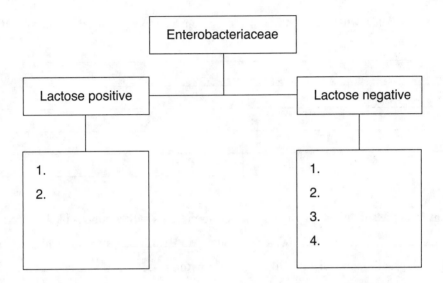

```
                    Enterobacteriaceae

   Lactose positive                      Lactose negative

      1.                                     1.
      2.                                     2.
                                            3.
                                            4.
```

5. Lactose fermentation is detected on _____ agar and lactose positive bacteria appear _____ on this agar.

6. Fill in the designation for the Enterobacteriaceae antigens from the descriptions in the table.

| Description | Antigen Designation |
| --- | --- |
| Flagella | |
| Capsule | |
| Outer membrane | |

7. List the lab characteristics that would differentiate between *Salmonella* and *Shigella* in a patient with bloody diarrhea.

Infectious Disease

8.  List the 2 lab characteristics that would be important in a patient with staghorn renal calculi.


9.  Fill in the table below with the most important virulence factors for the organisms listed.

| Organism | Most Important Virulence Factor |
|---|---|
| ETEC | |
| EHEC | |
| EUEC | |
| *(E) coli* strains that cause meningitis | |


10. A patient from the southwestern United States who presents with a bubo is likely infected with

    _____, which exhibits _____ staining, whereas a child who

    presents with pseudo-appendicitis is likely infected with _____, which

    can grow at 4° (C)


11. A patient with a duodenal ulcer is likely infected with _____. The stan-
    dard treatment for this is a multi-drug regiment involving _____. This
    patient is also at risk for 2 types of cancer. List the two.


12. Fill in the table with a "W" for watery or a "B" for bloody depending on the type of diarrhea
    caused by the agent listed to the left.

| Organism | Type of Diarrhea |
|---|---|
| *Vibrio cholerae* | |
| *Campylobacter jejuni* | |
| *Vibrio parahaemolyticus* | |
| *Vibrio vulnificus* | |

Infectious Disease

13. Name the mode of transmission for *Legionella pneumophila*.

14. _____ normally causes pneumonia in _____ patients, who tend to aspirate the organisms. The sputum would be described as _____.

15. Fill in the blanks in the table below regarding *Pseudomonas aeruginosa*.

| Properties (list at least 2) | | |
|---|---|---|
| Distinguishing features | | |
| Important virulence factors | | |
| Diseases (list 2 for each category): | | |
| Immune compromised | | |
| Otherwise healthy | | |
| **Treatment** | | |

16. Fill in the table with an "A" if the listed organism is aerobic or "AN" if the listed organism is anaerobic.

| Organism | Oxygen Requirement |
|---|---|
| *Actinomyces* | |
| *Bacillus* | |
| *Mycobacterium tuberculosis* | |
| *Bacteroides* | |
| *Pseudomonas* | |
| *Nocardia* | |
| *Clostridium* | |

Infectious Disease

## TOPIC 5: NON-GRAM STAINING ORGANISMS

1. Fill in the table below regarding *Mycobacterium tuberculosis*.

| Property | Mycobacterium tuberculosis |
|---|---|
| Primary disease (list characteristic finding) | |
| Secondary disease (reactivation) | |
| Triad of symptoms | |

2. A giant cell found in a granulomatous lesion in a TB patient is which cell type?

3. List 2 reasons a patient would test positive on a PPD test.

4. An AIDS patient with a CD4 T cell count of <50 cells/mm³ is susceptible to which mycobacterial disease?

5. List the natural reservoir for *Mycobacterium leprae* in the United States.

6. List the 2 types of diseases a patient can get when exposed to *Mycobacterium leprae*.

7. The diagnostic test for *Mycoplasma pneumoniae* is the _____.
   Beta-lactams don't work for treating this organism because it doesn't have _____.

8. List the spirochetes in order of size.

9. Draw a line from each organism to its correct mode of transmission.

Borrelia                 Sexual /contact birth

Treponema                Water contaminated with animal urine

Leptospira               Tick bite

10. Fill in the major symptoms for each listed stage of Lyme disease.

| Stage of Disease | Major Symptoms |
|---|---|
| Primary | |
| Secondary | |
| Tertiary | |

11. For each symptom listed for the stages of syphilis, fill in a "1" if it occurs in primary, "2" if it occurs in secondary, "3" if it occurs in tertiary, or "C" if it occurs in congenital.

| Symptom | Stage of Disease/Congenital |
|---|---|
| Gummas | |
| Alopecia | |
| Aortitis | |
| Tabes dorsalis | |
| Copper-colored rash | |
| Chancre (painless) | |
| Condylomata lata | |
| Argyll Robertson pupils | |
| Hutchinson teeth | |

Infectious Disease

12. The primary screening test for syphilis is the _____ test, and the confirmatory test is the _____.

13. Identify the animal associated with the infection produced by the organisms below.

| Organism | Animal |
|---|---|
| *Bartonella henselae* | |
| *Brucella abortus* | |
| *Francisella tularensis* | |
| *Pasteurella multocida* | |

14. A patient who develops a rash after a tick bite that spreads peripherally and moves centrally is likely infected with _____.

15. A patient who develops a rash after a body louse infestation that spreads centrally and moves peripherally is likely infected with _____.

16. Rickettsial diseases can be diagnosed by the _____, which takes advantage of a cross-reaction of rickettsial antigens with non-motile strains of _____.

17. The organisms in the genus *Chlamydia* are obligate intracellular because they can't make their own _____. The infectious form of the organism is known as the _____, whereas the replicative form is known as the _____.

18. A patient treated for *Chlamydia trachomatis* (serotypes D-K) should also be treated for _____.

19. For each chlamydial disease listed in the table, put a "T" if it is caused by *(C) trachomatis*, a "PN" if it is caused by *(C) pneumophila,* or a "PS" if it is caused by *(C) psittaci.*

| Disease | Chlamydia Species |
|---|---|
| Pelvic inflammatory disease | |
| Trachoma | |
| Parrot fever | |
| Lymphogranuloma venereum | |
| Walking pneumonia | |

20. For each disease caused by *Chlamydia trachomatis* listed in the table, fill in the appropriate serotypes that are responsible for the diseases.

| Disease | Serotypes |
|---|---|
| Trachoma | |
| Non-gonococcal urethritis | |
| Neonatal conjunctivitis | |
| Lymphogranuloma venereum | |

Infectious Disease

## TOPIC 6: MYCOLOGY

1. Mammalian cells have _____ in the cell membrane, whereas fungi have _____ in the cell membranes.

2. List the 3 genera of fungi that appear in cutaneous fungal infections.

3. Cutaneous fungal infections are always monomorphic and in the _____. A _____ is used to diagnose these types of infections.

4. Tinea versicolor is caused by _____ and appears as _____ on the skin.

   A KOH mount would reveal a _____.

5. For each organism listed below, fill in the geographic distribution and description of the yeast form.

| Organism | Geography | Yeast Form |
|---|---|---|
| *Sporothrix schenckii* | N/A | |
| *Histoplasma capsulatum* | | |
| *Blastomyces dermatitidis* | | |
| *Coccidioides immitis* | | |
| *Paracoccidioides brasiliensis* | | |

6.  For the different patient populations listed, write in the diseases that *Candida* can cause in each.

| Patient Population | Diseases |
|---|---|
| AIDS | |
| Diabetic | |
| IV drug users | |

7.  Recurrent superficial *Candida* infections may suggest a defect in _____, whereas recurrent systemic infections may suggest a defect in _____.

8.  *Aspergillus* infections can be diagnosed by finding _____ hyphae at _____ angles.

9.  *Cryptococcus neoformans* is a monomorphic _____ with a large _____ that stains with India ink.

10. *Pneumocystis jiroveci* is most commonly found in which patient population? _____

11. *Mucor* infections can be diagnosed by finding _____ hyphae at _____ angles.

## TOPIC 7: PARASITOLOGY

1. Place an "X" under the property that corresponds to the organisms listed in the table.

| Organism | Acid Fast | Found in Hikers | Liver Abscesses | Bloody Diarrhea | Malabsorption | Chronic Diarrhea in AIDS Patients |
|---|---|---|---|---|---|---|
| *Giardia lamblia* | | | | | | |
| *Entamoeba histolytica* | | | | | | |
| *Cryptosporidium parvum* | | | | | | |

2. For each of the diseases/symptoms/findings caused by *Toxoplasma gondii*, place an "I" if it occurs in immuncompromised patients or a "C" if congenital.

| Disease/Symptoms/Findings | Patient Population |
|---|---|
| Chorioretinitis | |
| Encephalitis/ring-enhancing lesions | |
| Brain abscess | |
| Hydrocephalus | |

3. Fill in the insect vectors for the following parasites.

| Parasite | Vector |
|---|---|
| *Trypanosoma brucei* | |
| *Trypanosoma cruzi* | |
| *Leishmania* | |

Infectious Disease

4. Fill in the geography, RBC forms, and vector for the organisms listed in the table.

| Organism | Geography | RBC Forms | Vector |
|---|---|---|---|
| *Plasmodium falciparum* | | | |
| *Babesia microti* | | | |

5. A patient with foul-smelling frothy green vaginal discharge would likely have

   _____ on a wet mount and an infection with

   _____. Treatment for this patient is _____.

6. Fill in the common names and major symptoms for the organisms listed in the table.

| Organism | Common Name | Major Symptom |
|---|---|---|
| *Diphyllobothrium latum* | | |
| *Echinococcus granulosus* | | |

7. Fill in the mode of transmission for each disease listed below caused by *Taenia solium*.

| Disease | Mode of Transmission |
|---|---|
| Cysticercosis | |
| Intestinal tapeworm | |

8. *Necator americanus* (or *Ancylostoma*) parasites are acquired via _____.

   The symptoms of hookworm infections are usually _____.

9.  Fill in the appropriate parasite for each diagnostic stage listed in the table.

| Diagnostic Stage (Egg) | Parasite |
|---|---|
| Tire-shaped egg | |
| Egg with flattened side, larvae inside | |
| Football-shaped egg with bipolar plugs | |
| Eggs with knobby coat | |

10. Fill in the mode of transmission for each of the parasites listed.

| Parasite | Mode of Transmission |
|---|---|
| *Trichinella spiralis* | |
| *Dracunculus medinensis* | |
| *Loa loa* | |
| *Wuchereria bancrofti* | |
| *Toxocara canis* | |
| *Onchocerca volvulus* | |

11. For the following parasites, list their target site of infection:

*Paragonimus westermani*  _____

*Clonorchis sinensis*  _____

*Schistosoma haematobium*  _____

*Schistosoma mansoni*  _____

## TOPIC 8: DNA VIRUSES

1.  The viral envelope is typically derived from the _____, whereas herpes viruses utilize the _____ for their envelope.

2.  List the 2 types of common viral capsid symmetries.

3.  For each number listed, list the step in viral replication that is occurring.

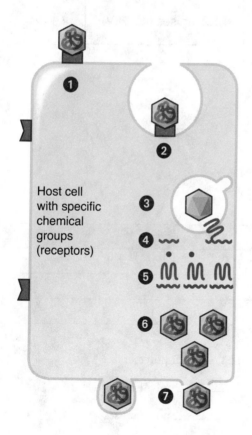

Host cell with specific chemical groups (receptors)

1) _____

2) _____

3) _____

4) _____

5) _____

6) _____

7) _____

Infectious Disease

4.  Using the cell diagram below, draw lines to where each of the different viruses listed replicates.

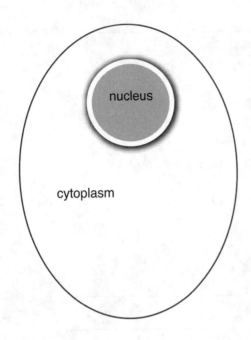

```
Most DNA viruses


Poxvirus


RNA viruses (not HIV)
```

5.  Complete the following table regarding replication of viruses.

| Virus Type (Genome) | Replicative Intermediate | Progeny Genome |
|---|---|---|
| DNA viruses | | |
| Positive stranded RNA | | |
| Negative stranded RNA | | |

6.  RNA viruses use an _____ dependent _____ polymerase.

DNA viruses use a _____ dependent _____ polymerase.

Retroviruses use an _____ dependent _____ polymerase.

7. For each infectious agent listed, add the type of viral infection: abortive, cytolytic, or persistent.

| Virus | Type of Viral Infection |
|---|---|
| Poliovirus | |
| Adenovirus in hamsters | |
| HBV or HCV | |
| HSV-1 or HSV-2 | |

8. For each virus listed, put an "L" if the agent has a live vaccine, "K" if the agent has a killed vaccine, or "R" if the agent has a recombinant vaccine. Note that some agents have >1 vaccine available and can have >1 designation.

| Virus | Vaccine Type |
|---|---|
| Measles, mumps, rubella | |
| Hepatitis A virus | |
| Influenza | |
| Polio | |
| Hepatitis B virus | |
| Human papillomavirus | |
| Varicella-zoster virus | |

9. The only ss DNA virus is _____. ALL others are ds.

10. The only DNA virus that replicates in the cytoplasm is _____; all others replicate in the nucleus.

11. Fill in the following categories for the herpesviruses listed.

| Virus | Clinical Presentation of Primary Infection | Site of Latency | Clinical Presentation and Site of Reactivation |
|-------|------|------|------|
| HSV-1 | | | |
| HSV-2 | | | |
| VZV | | | |
| EBV | | | |
| CMV | | | |

12. Describe the heterophile antibody test and what it is used for.

13. For each disease listed, put "C" if it is caused by CMV, "E" if it is caused by EBV, or "B" if it can be caused by both.

| Disease | Viral Cause |
|---------|-------------|
| Mononucleosis in a teenager | |
| Interstitial pneumonia in an immunocompromised patient | |
| Retinitis in an AIDS patient | |
| Burkitt lymphoma | |

14. Which of the following cases best describes roseola?

(A) A 10-year-old develops an asynchronous vesicular rash

(B) A 3-month-old develops a high fever for 3 days, the fever goes away, a lacy body rash appears

(C) A 14-year-old develops cough, coryza, conjunctivitis, and a maculopapular rash

15. Kaposi sarcoma is associated with what co-morbidity?

16. For each characteristic listed, put a "B" if it is characteristic of HBV, a "C" if it is characteristic of HCV, or "both" if the characteristic applies to both viruses.

| Characteristic | Virus |
|---|---|
| Uses reverse transcriptase in replication | |
| DNA virus | |
| RNA virus | |
| More often causes chronic hepatitis | |
| More often causes acute hepatitis | |
| Cirrhosis/liver cancer | |
| Blood borne/sexually transmitted | |

17. List at least 2 diseases caused by adenovirus.

18. List the 2 patient populations at high risk for severe infection with B19 virus.

19. For each disease listed, provide the appropriate virus family.

| Disease | Viral Family |
|---|---|
| Genital warts | |
| Vaccinia | |
| Molluscum contagiosum | |
| Progressive multifocal leukoencephalopathy | |

20. For each viral family listed, put a "+" if the virus family is positive stranded or "–" if the virus family is negative stranded. Also, put an "X" if the viral family is segmented.

| Viral Family | Genome Type + or – Stranded RNA | Segmented Genome |
|---|---|---|
| Retroviridae | | |
| Orthomyxoviridae | | |
| Paramyxoviridae | | |
| Reoviridae | | |
| Caliciviridae | | |
| Picornaviridae | | |
| Bunyaviridae | | |
| Togaviridae | | |
| Rhabdoviridae | | |
| Flaviviridae | | |
| Arenaviridae | | |

# TOPIC 9: RNA VIRUSES

1. Name the mode of transmission for picornaviruses.


2. Name the mode of transmission for flaviviruses.


3. Name the most common cause of pediatric gastroenteritis in the United States.


4. What is the function of the influenza hemagglutinin (HA) glycoprotein?


5. What is the function of the influenza neuraminidase (NA) glycoprotein?


6. For each description regarding influenza viruses, put "shift" if it describes antigenic shift or "drift" if it describes antigenic drift.

| Description | Antigenic Shift or Antigenic Drift |
| --- | --- |
| Influenza pandemics | |
| Influenza epidemics | |
| Random mutations in HA or NA | |
| Complete viral assortment | |

7. Describe the rash caused by rubella virus in a child or adult.

Infectious Disease

8.  The major concern about a primary infection with rubella virus during pregnancy is:

9.  List the 4 major viruses in the paramyxovirus family.

10. All paramyxoviruses have a _____ protein in their viral envelope, which leads to the formation of _____ from cell:cell fusion.

11. The major symptom of infection with mumps virus in a child is _____.

12. List 2 serious sequelae of infection with mumps.

13. List the top 3 animals associated with rabies transmission in the United States.

14. Describe the mechanism of spread of rabies virus from a bite wound on the leg to the brain.

15. List 3 viral families associated with arboviral transmission.

16. For each hepatitis virus, put an "X" where the listed trait applies to that virus.

| Hepatitis Virus | Fecal–Oral Transmission | Blood borne/ Sexual Transmission | DNA Virus | RNA Virus | Associated with Chronicity |
|---|---|---|---|---|---|
| HAV | | | | | |
| HBV | | | | | |
| HCV | | | | | |
| HDV | | | | | |
| HEV | | | | | |

17. For each description, write the HBV Ag or Ab that is appropriate.

- Provides immunity to HBV. _____

- Important for screening recent infections. _____

- If found in the blood past 6 months of first screening, indicative of a chronic infection with HBV. _____

- If found indicates virus is easily transmitted. _____

18. Label the following drawing of HIV virus for the following: gp41, gp120, p24, and genome.

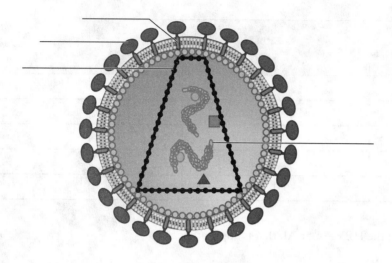

19. List the screening and confirmatory tests for HIV.

20. List the progressive stages of HIV.

21. List the HIV-associated neoplasms and virus associated with them (if applicable).

22. Prions are what type of pathogen?

Infectious Disease

23. How is Creutzfeldt-Jakob disease transmitted?

24. List the agents that comprise the TORCHES.

## TOPIC 10: ANTIBACTERIALS

1. Complete the diagram below for cell wall synthesis inhibitors.

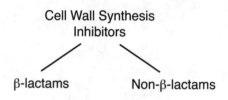

_____  _____  _____  _____      _____

2. Identify the generation of cephalosporin.

| Drug | Generation |
|------|------------|
| Cefaclor | |
| Cefepime | |
| Ceftriaxone | |
| Cefotaxime | |
| Cephalexin | |

3. Clavulanic acid is often combined with amoxicillin because _____.

4.  What type of bacteria are killed by vancomycin?

5.  Match each drug listed with its ribosomal target.

| Drug | Target |
|---|---|
| Chloramphenicol | |
| Doxycycline | |
| Gentamicin | |
| Clarithromycin | |
| Clindamycin | |
| Linezolid | |

6.  What antibiotic has its main use as a treatment for SIADH?

7.  What 2 types of antibiotics are commonly used against atypical organisms such as chlamydia and mycoplasma?

8. Add the antibiotic or antibiotic drug class most likely associated with the side effect listed.

| Side Effect | Drug |
|---|---|
| Gray baby syndrome | |
| Ototoxicity | |
| Tooth discoloration | |
| Red man syndrome | |
| Hemolytic anemia | |
| Tendonitis | |
| Disulfiram reaction | |

9. Using one of the following, classify each drug according to its mechanism.

CW = cell wall inhibitor        PSI = protein synthesis

AF = antifolate                      DNA = DNA or nucleic acid synthesis inhibitor

| Drug | Mechanism |
|---|---|
| Ciprofloxacin | |
| TMP-SMX | |
| Penicillin G | |
| Azithromycin | |
| Vancomycin | |
| Doxycycline | |
| Metronidazole | |
| Cefazolin | |

10. Increased bacterial production of PABA may confer resistance to what type of antibiotic?

11. Complete the mnemonic for a list of important TB drugs.

     **R** _____

     **E** _____

     **S** _____

     **P** _____

     **I** _____

     r

     e

12. Bacterial conversion of the terminal d-alanine to d-lactate confers resistance to what drug?

## TOPIC 11: OTHER ANTIBIOTICS

1. Match the antifungal drug or drug class with the listed target.

| Drug | Target |
|------|--------|
|      | Thymidylate synthase |
|      | Microtubule formation |
|      | Ergosterol |
|      | β-glucan synthesis |
|      | Ergosterol synthesis |
|      | Squalene epoxidase |

2. What enzyme, present in influenza A and B, is targeted by oseltamivir?

3. Activation of antiherpetic drugs such as acyclovir and ganciclovir require what viral enzyme?

4. What antiherpetic drug does not require the enzyme from the previous question?

5. Match each drug listed to the virus it targets. Use the last 4 letters of each drug name to help guide you.

| Drug | Target |
|------|--------|
| Oseltamivir |  |
| Ganciclovir |  |
| Ritonavir |  |
| Acyclovir |  |
| Indinavir |  |
| Zanamivir |  |

6. Complete the table below for antiretroviral drugs.

| Drug | Target |
|---|---|
| Zidovudine | |
| Ritonavir | |
| | Gp41 |
| Efavirenz | |

7. For each sexually transmitted disease listed, identify the antimicrobial most likely to be used.

| Disease/Cause | Drug |
|---|---|
| *Chlamydia* | |
| *Trichomonas* | |
| *Gardnerella vaginosis* | |
| Syphilis | |
| Gonorrhea | |

# CHAPTER 5

# EPIDEMIOLOGY AND BIOSTATISTICS

## TOPIC 1: EPIDEMIOLOGY

1. When comparing the actual cases to the number of potential cases in the determination of rate, the potential cases would be in the _____ and the actual cases would be in the _____.

2. Rates are generally expressed per _____ (number) of persons with the exception of vital statistics, which are expressed per _____ (number) of persons.

3. Complete the following equation:

    Incidence rate = _____

4. What type of 'cases' should be excluded in the calculation of incidence rate?

5. What type of 'cases' should be excluded in the calculation of attack rate?

6. The attack rate is defined as _____.

7. Complete the following equation:

   Prevalence rate = _____

8. What is the difference between point prevalence and period prevalence?

9. When incidence increases, then prevalence usually _____.

10. Prevalence = Incidence × _____

11. Complete the following table with "no change," "increase," or "decrease."

| What is the change to incidence and prevalence when: | Incidence | Prevalence |
|---|---|---|
| A new vaccine for a condition becomes available | | |
| Long-term survival rates for a disease are decreasing | | |
| A formerly effective medication is becoming ineffective due to widespread resistance | | |
| Number of persons dying from a condition are increasing | | |
| A new effective treatment is available | | |

12.  Complete the table with the appropriate information on phases of a clinical trial.

| | Phase I | Phase II | Phase III | Phase IV |
|---|---|---|---|---|
| Type of patients in sample | Healthy individuals (20 – 100) | Patients with disease (100-300) | Patients with disease (100s-1000s) | Patients with disease (1000s) |
| Data evaluated | | | | |
| Duration | 1 – 30 days | Months | Months to years | |

13.  Cohort studies are observational studies in which subjects are classified as either having or not having a _____ and then followed _____ in time.

14.  Data from cohort studies are usually analyzed by means of _____ calculations to estimate the increase in incidence due to the presence of that risk factor.

15.  Case-control studies identify individuals with disease, then go back in time to identify _____ that might be associated with a given disease or condition.

16.  Data from case-control studies are usually analyzed by means of _____.

17.  Cross-sectional studies assess the _____ of a disease in a given population and what factors are associated with having that disease.

18.  In cross-sectional studies, association of identified factors with disease is usually assessed by using _____.

19. Crossover studies are clinical trials in which 2 comparison groups _____ receive the study drug and the comparative intervention but at _____ times.

20. A crossover study will begin with one study group receiving _____, while a comparison (control) group receives _____. Then, at some predetermined point, the first group is _____, while the second group is _____.

21. Given the following 2 × 2 table, add TP (true positive), FP (false positive), FN (false negative), and TN (true negative).

| | Disease Present | Disease Absent |
|---|---|---|
| **Screening Test Results Positive** | | |
| **Screening Test Results Negative** | | |

22. Based on the 2 × 2 table, what is the specificity for this test?

23. Based on the 2 × 2 table, what is the sensitivity for this test?

24. Based on the 2 × 2 table, what is the positive predictive value for this test?

25. Based on the 2 × 2 table, what is the negative predictive value for this test?

26. Explain what SNOUT means.

27. Explain what SPIN means.

28. A meta-analysis is a statistical way of combining the results of many studies to produce

_____.

29. A meta-analysis will increase _____.

30. A meta-analysis can be limited by what 2 factors?

31. A meta-analysis will help to eliminate what kind of bias?

32. What is the difference between accuracy and precision?

33. Is validity matched with accuracy or precision?

34. For the diagram below, what can be said with respect to accuracy and precision?

35. What type of error reduces the accuracy in a test?

36. What type of error reduces the precision in a test?

37. For the table below, identify which patients have been exposed to the risk factor and which patients have not.

|  | Disease Present | Disease Absent |
|---|---|---|
| Risk Factor (+) | A | B |
| Risk Factor (−) | C | D |

38. For the table above, how would the relative risk and attributable risk (cohort studies) be calculated?

39. Which of the following yields a p-value?

    (A)    Absolute risk reduction

    (B)    Attributable risk

    (C)    Number needed to treat

    (D)    Odds ratio

    (E)    Relative risk

40. NNT is the number of patients who need to be treated for _____ patient to benefit.

41. Relative risk and attributable risk tell us that there are statistical differences, but they do not tell us

    _____.

42. The Hawthorne effect is what type of bias?

43. The Pygmalion effect is what type of bias?

44. Recall bias is primarily seen in what types of research studies?

45. Combining the results from multiple studies is a way to prevent what kind of bias?

    (A)    Confounding bias

    (B)    Design bias

    (C)    Late look bias

    (D)    Recall bias

46. To prevent design bias, researchers could do which of the following?

    (A)  Conformation

    (B)  Meta-analysis

    (C)  Random assignment

    (D)  Stratify by disease severity

47. A new screening test is developed that identifies a fatal disease earlier. Researchers soon report that patients with that particular disease are living longer. This is an example of _____ bias. This type of bias causes the reporting of _____. How could researchers prevent this type of bias?

# TOPIC 2: BIOSTATISTICS

1. The null hypothesis is considered to be the _____ of what a researcher is hoping to prove.

2. If a researcher wants to reject the null hypothesis, she must have a p-value of less than or equal to

   _____.

3. If a researcher is able to obtain the desired p-value (in question 2), it means that

   _____ has been achieved.

4. In the statistical testing of a hypothesis, the alternative hypothesis is _____ if the null
   hypothesis is _____.

5. In statistical hypothesis testing, researchers never do what to the null hypothesis?

   (A)  Accept it

   (B)  Fail to reject it

   (C)  Reject it

   (D)  Researchers can do all of the above

6. Researchers want to investigate the claim that the normal arterial pH is *not* between 7.35 and 7.45.
   The null hypothesis is _____. The alternative null hypothesis is

   _____.

7. Define an alpha error.

8. If the p-value is 0.04, then the chance of committing a _____ error is _____.

9. If a type II error is an error of omission, then a type I error is an error of _____.

10. A research study is evaluating the effectiveness of a new powerful antimicrobial agent godzillacil-lin. When comparing godzillacillin to amoxicillin/clavulanic acid for the treatment of a specific infection, researchers achieve a p-value of 0.0001.

    Were researchers able to prove that godzillacillin is more effective than amoxicillin/clavulanic acid with absolute certainty? _____ Why?

11. The results of a landmark placebo-controlled, randomized clinical trial study are published.

    Which would be worse for the general population, the researchers committing a type 1 or type 2 error? _____ Why?

12. If researchers are able to obtain a p-value of 0.001 in a drug study, this p-value does not prove which of the following?

    (A) Clinical relevance

    (B) Statistical significance

    (C) Both A and B are proven with this p-value

    (D) Both A and B are not proven with this p-value

13. Power is directly related to a type _____ error and is most commonly increased when a researcher is able to increase _____.

14. The most frequently occurring value in a set of observations is known as the _____.

Epidemiology and Biostatistics

15. What type of "skew" is occurring when the mean < median < mode? _____

16. For the following set of numbers (3, 6, 6, 7, 9, 10, 12), what is the mean, median, and mode, respectively?

17. In a normal distribution curve, what percent of cases are above 2 standard deviations below the mean? Provide your calculation.

18. If 1.0 is not included in the confidence interval, then what are researchers able to assume?

19. Complete the table below.

| Variables | | | |
|---|---|---|---|
| Name of Statistical Test | Interval | Nominal | Number of groups? |
| | 0 | 2 | Any number of groups |
| One-way ANOVA | | | 2 or more groups |
| | 1 | 1 | 2 groups only |
| Pearson Correlation | | | |

20. Prevention of a disease from occurring is an example of which of the following?

    (A)  Primary prevention

    (B)  Secondary prevention

    (C)  Tertiary prevention

    (D)  Treatment measure

21. Obtaining a PSA in an elderly male is an example of which of the following?

    (A)   Primary prevention

    (B)   Secondary prevention

    (C)   Tertiary prevention

    (D)   Treatment measure

22. The use of an antibiotic in a child with an ear infection is an example of which of the following?

    (A)   Primary prevention

    (B)   Secondary prevention

    (C)   Tertiary prevention

    (D)   Treatment measure

23. The use of abacavir + lamivudine + efavirenz in an HIV infected female is an example of which of the following?

    (A)   Primary prevention

    (B)   Secondary prevention

    (C)   Tertiary prevention

    (D)   Treatment measure

24. A 23-year-old sexually active female requiring her partner to wear a condom is an example of which of the following?

    (A)   Primary prevention

    (B)   Secondary prevention

    (C)   Tertiary prevention

    (D)   Treatment measure

25. If a patient has HIV, reporting to state and local authorities varies depending on
    _____. However, HIV is reportable _____.

26. Which of the following should be reported?

    (A)  AIDS

    (B)  Hepatitis A

    (C)  MMR

    (D)  All of the above

27. The leading causes of death in children ages 1–14 years are _____.

28. Cancer, heart disease, and injuries are the leading causes of death in people of what age range?

29. Women attempt suicide _____ times as often as men.

30. Suicides outnumber _____ in the United States as a cause of death.

31. Approximately how many suicide attempts are there for every one that succeeds?

    (A)  2–5

    (B)  5–10

    (C)  10–20

    (D)  20–50

    (E)  75–100

32. Medicare and Medicaid receive their funding from _____.

33. At what age are people eligible for Medicare?

    (A)  Any age

    (B)  >50 years

    (C)  >60 years

    (D)  >65 years

34. What are the criteria to be eligible for Medicaid?



35. Medical residents receive their salaries from _____.



36. Salaries for medical residents across the United States are _____ because _____.

# BEHAVIORAL MEDICINE AND ETHICS

## TOPIC 1: CHILD AND ADOLESCENT DEVELOPMENT

1.  Complete the following table for the APGAR scoring system.

| APGAR Scoring System | | | |
| --- | --- | --- | --- |
| Evaluation | 0 Points | 1 Point | 2 Points |
| Heart rate | 0 | <____/min | >____/min |
| Respiration | None | | |
| Color | | Pale, blue extremities | |
| Tone | | | Active |
| Reflex irritability | None | | |

2.  Low birth weight is considered anything less than _____ kg.

3.  APGAR stands for _____.

4.  A young girl should be able to copy a triangle at what age? _____

5. An infant should be expected to change hands when playing with a toy at what age?

   _____

6. At what age would a young boy be expected to turn a doorknob, imitate mannerisms, and parallel play? _____

7. At what age would a child be expected to conform to peers, ask the meaning of words, and have a brain weight of approximately 75% of that of an adult? _____

8. At what age would a child be expected to use approximately 900 words and stack 9 cubes?

   _____

9. Describe the social development expectations for a 4-year-old boy.

10. Complete the following table for the Tanner stages of development.

| Tanner Stages of Development | | | |
|---|---|---|---|
| **Stage** | **Female Breast** | **Female and Male Pubic Hair** | **Male Genitalia** |
| 1 | Preadolescent | None | |
| 2 | | | Enlargement of scrotum/testes |
| 3 | | | |
| 4 | | Coarse, curly, adult type | |
| 5 | Mature female | | Adult shape/size |

11. At what age would the pubic hair in a female or male be described as coarse and curly?

      _____

12. What are the 3 major causes of sexual dysfunction in a man who is NOT diagnosed with erectile dysfunction?

      (A) _____

      (B) _____

      (C) _____

13. What effect does stress have on cortisol levels, cholesterol levels, and immune function, respectively?


14. BMI is a measure of _____ adjusted for _____, and is calculated as follows:


15. A BMI of _____ is considered to be normal.


16. A BMI of _____ is considered to be obese.


17. A BMI of _____ should be treated with diet and _____.

Behavioral Medicine and Ethics

## TOPIC 2: GERIATRIC HEALTH AND GRIEF

1. Which of the following is decreased in the elderly?

   (A) Percentage body fat

   (B) Intelligence

   (C) Sexual interest

   (D) All of the above

   (E) None of the above

2. The sexually related changes that occur in men and women, respectively, are

   _____ and

   _____.

3. With respect to sleep patterns in the elderly, one would expect to see _____ REM and slow-wave sleep and _____ latency and awakenings.

4. Men from the ages of _____ have the highest suicide rate in the United States.

5. A physician would expect to see _____ volume of distribution for highly lipid-soluble drugs in the elderly. Explain your answer.

6. Grief can last up to _____ months and should be treated if it lasts more than _____ months.

7. What are the 5 stages of grief according to Kubler-Ross? _____

8. Do the 5 stages of grief in the Kubler-Ross model have to appear in a certain order to be classified as "normal" grief? _____

9. Are antidepressants indicated for individuals experiencing normal grief? _____

10. Crying, decreased libido, weight loss, and insomnia are common in which of the following?

    (A)   Depression
    (B)   Normal grief
    (C)   Prolonged grief
    (D)   All of the above
    (E)   None of the above

Behavioral Medicine and Ethics

# TOPIC 3: SLEEP AND SLEEP DISORDERS

1.  The circadian rhythm is controlled by _____.

2.  Beta waves would predominate on an EEG in what sleep stages? _____

3.  What is the main neurotransmitter in REM sleep? _____

4.  Which of the following should be treated with amphetamine salts?

    (A)  Depression

    (B)  Enuresis

    (C)  Narcolepsy

    (D)  Sleep disorder in depressed patients

    (E)  Sleep terror disorder

5.  What is the difference between the sleep stages in night terrors and nightmares?

6.  Fill in the blanks in the table below with "increase," "decrease," or "no change."

| Sleep Patterns of Patients with Major Depression | | | |
|---|---|---|---|
| Slow wave sleep | REM early in sleep cycle | REM latency | Total REM sleep |
|  |  |  |  |

7.  What are the recommended treatment measures for sleep apnea syndromes?

8. What increases the risk for sudden infant death syndrome?

9. What are the differences between the sleep stages for somnambulism and bruxism?

10. Which of the following is indicated for the treatment of chronic enuresis?

   (A) Amphetamine salts
   (B) Desmopressin
   (C) Diphenhydramine
   (D) Imipramine
   (E) Octreotide

# TOPIC 4: INTRODUCTION TO PSYCHIATRIC DISORDERS

1.  A 36-year-old female is diagnosed with generalized anxiety disorder. Her condition would be classified under which of the following Axes?

    (A)  Axis I

    (B)  Axis II

    (C)  Axis III

    (D)  Axis IV

    (E)  Axis V

2.  What are the primary Axis II disorders?

3.  A patient with Down syndrome is described as being "trainable and would benefit from vocational training but needs adult supervision." What would be his expected IQ range? _____

4.  Match the defense mechanism on the left with the appropriate definition or important association on the right.

    (A)  Acting out              _____ Attributing inner feelings to others

    (B)  Altruism                _____ The world is composed of polar opposites

    (C)  Blocking                _____ Substance abuse, reaction to death

    (D)  Denial                  _____ Transient ability to remember

    (E)  Isolation of affect     _____ Unconscious, indirect hostility

    (F)  Passive-aggressive      _____ Enuresis, primitive behaviors

    (G)  Projection              _____ Forget and remember

    (H)  Reaction formation _____ Moving an improper impulse into an acceptable channel

    (I)  Regression              _____ Affect covered up by excessive action or sensation

    (J)  Sublimation             _____ The unacceptable transformed into its opposite

    (K)  Splitting               _____ Guilt is alleviated by unsolicited generosity to others

    (L)  Suppression             _____ Facts without feelings

5. A 62-year-old woman is scheduled to have a colonoscopy and administered 10 mg of diazepam. This medication is likely to cause what type of amnesia?

    (A)  Anterograde amnesia

    (B)  Dissociative amnesia

    (C)  Korsakoff's amnesia

    (D)  Retrograde amnesia

6. A patient with Korsakoff's amnesia is likely to be deficient in which of the following vitamins?

    (A)  Vitamin B1

    (B)  Vitamin B3

    (C)  Vitamin B6

    (D)  Vitamin B12

    (E)  Vitamin K

7. Cognitive disorders are associated with significant changes in what?


8. Label the following as delirium or dementia:

    (A)  _____ Insidious onset

    (B)  _____ Visual hallucinations more common

    (C)  _____ Associated with less sleep disruption

    (D)  _____ Attention span generally not decreased

    (E)  _____ Reversible condition

    (F)  _____ Duration is generally days to weeks

    (G)  _____ Remote memories seem as recent memories


9. Can patients with dementia develop delirium? _____

10. Explain the relationship (if one exists) between illicit drug abuse and both delirium and dementia.

11. Fill in the missing neurotransmitter in the table below.

| Disorder | Neurotransmitter Changes | |
|---|---|---|
| Alzheimer's disease | Inc: | |
| | Dec: | |
| Anxiety | Inc: | |
| | Dec: | |
| Depression | Inc: | |
| | Dec: | |
| Huntington's disease | Inc: | |
| | Dec: | |
| Parkinson's disease | Inc: | |
| | Dec: | |
| Schizophrenia | Inc: | |
| | Dec: | |

## TOPIC 5: CHILDHOOD AND PERVASIVE DISORDERS

1.  Prolonged affection deprivation in an infant generally leads to all of the following *except*:

    (A)  Anaclitic depression

    (B)  Decreased muscle tone

    (C)  Increased trust of other adults

    (D)  Poor socialization skills

    (E)  Weight loss

    (F)  Affection deprivation leads to all of the above

2.  All of the following must be reported to the proper authorities upon discovery by a physician *except*:

    (A)  Child neglect

    (B)  Physical abuse (child)

    (C)  Physical abuse (spouse)

    (D)  Sexual abuse (child)

    (E)  All of the above must be reported by a physician

3.  Antipsychotic medications are most commonly used in the treatment of which of the following?

    (A)  ADHD

    (B)  Conduct disorder

    (C)  Oppositional defiant disorder

    (D)  Separation anxiety disorder

    (E)  Tourette's syndrome

Behavioral Medicine and Ethics

4.  Methylphenidate is most commonly used in the treatment of which of the following?

    (A)  ADHD

    (B)  Conduct disorder

    (C)  Oppositional defiant disorder

    (D)  Separation anxiety disorder

    (E)  Tourette's syndrome

5.  Continual pattern of defiant and hostile behavior toward authority figures is most commonly seen in patients with which of the following?

    (A)  ADHD

    (B)  Conduct disorder

    (C)  Oppositional defiant disorder

    (D)  Separation anxiety disorder

    (E)  Tourette's syndrome

6.  Motor and vocal tics are commonly seen in patients diagnosed with

    _____.

7.  Provide examples of the vocal and motor tics in patients diagnosed with the condition in question 6.

8.  Describe the treatment of autism.

9.  With respect to intelligence, what is the difference between patients with Asperger's syndrome and autism?

10. Why is Rett's syndrome primarily seen in females?

# TOPIC 6: SCHIZOPHRENIA AND DISSOCIATIVE DISORDERS

1. Describe the difference between hallucinations and delusions.


2. Which of the following hallucinations are most commonly seen in schizophrenia?

   (A) Auditory

   (B) Gustatory

   (C) Olfactory

   (D) Tactile

   (E) Visual

   (F) All of the above are commonly seen in schizophrenia

3. Which of the following hallucinations are most commonly seen in alcohol withdrawal?

   (A) Auditory

   (B) Gustatory

   (C) Olfactory

   (D) Tactile

   (E) Visual

4. What is believed to be the primary cause of schizophrenia?

   (A) Decreased acetylcholine

   (B) Decreased dopamine

   (C) Decreased serotonin

   (D) Increased acetylcholine

   (E) Increased dopamine

   (F) Increased serotonin

5. Negative symptoms of schizophrenia include:

   (A)  Delusions

   (B)  Disorganized or catatonic behavior

   (C)  Disorganized speech

   (D)  Hallucinations

   (E)  Social withdrawal

   (F)  All of the above are negative symptoms of schizophrenia

6. Delusions of persecution or grandeur are primarily associated with which of the following sub-types of schizophrenia?

   (A)  Catatonic

   (B)  Disorganized

   (C)  Paranoid

   (D)  Residual

   (E)  Undifferentiated

7. What is the primary difference between high- and low-potency antipsychotics?

8. A patient experiencing repetitive movements of the lips, tongue, and limbs for the past 120 days is likely to be diagnosed with _____.

9. In addition to blocking the dopamine D2 receptors, olanzapine also acts as a _____ receptor antagonist.

10. Clozapine acts at the dopamine _____ receptor and is most commonly associated with the development of _____ which requires _____ monitoring of _____.

## TOPIC 7: MOOD DISORDERS

1. A mood disorder is characterized by a disturbance in the person's mood and _____ over that mood.

2. A milder form of bipolar disorder is _____.

3. Complete the following table on the symptoms of mania. Keep in mind the **DIG FAST** mnemonic.

| Symptom | Explanation |
|---|---|
|  | Inability to concentrate |
| Interest or irresponsibility |  |
|  | Inflated self-esteem |
|  |  |
| Appetite or agitation |  |
|  |  |
|  | Loud and pressured speech |

4. A 28-year-old man is diagnosed with bipolar disorder in which manic symptoms predominate. Which of the following would be indicated as initial therapy?

   (A) Clozapine

   (B) Electroconvulsive therapy

   (C) Ethosuximide

   (D) Fluoxetine

   (E) Olanzapine

5. A non-pregnant woman with bipolar disorder is treated with lithium. Which of the following is most likely to occur as a direct result of her therapy?

   (A) Ebstein's anomaly

   (B) Hyperthyroidism

   (C) Nephrogenic diabetes insipidus

   (D) All of the above could occur in this patient as a direct result of lithium therapy

6. Is fluoxetine indicated for the treatment of both dysthymia and seasonal affective disorder?

   _____ If not, then which condition should it be used to treat under what conditions?

7. According to the biogenic amine theory of depression, what 2 neurotransmitters are involved in major depression?

8. Side effects of the tricyclic antidepressants are primarily mediated through

   _____.

9. If a patient is taking phenelzine and drinks a glass of red wine while eating aged cheese, which of the following is likely to occur?

   (A) Hypertensive crisis

   (B) Neuroleptic malignant syndrome

   (C) Pulmonary fibrosis

   (D) Serotonin syndrome

10. Describe serotonin syndrome.

11. Venlafaxine acts by what mechanism?

12. A male patient taking trazodone should be concerned about which side effect?

   (A) Erectile dysfunction

   (B) Priapism

   (C) Seizures

   (D) All of the above

13. Electroconvulsive therapy is used in the treatment of depression in cases when

   _____.

## TOPIC 8: ANXIETY DISORDERS

1. An anxiety disorder is characterized by excessive _____ and is associated with _____ manifestations.

2. To make a diagnosis of generalized anxiety disorder, _____ out of 6 symptoms must be present. What are these possible symptoms?

   (A) _____

   (B) _____

   (C) _____

   (D) _____

   (E) _____

   (F) _____

3. Acute therapy for generalized anxiety disorder generally involves the use of _____.
   Long-term, first line therapy includes the use of _____.

4. Next to each drug below list its most common uses:

   (A) Alprazolam _____

   (B) Chlordiazepoxide _____

   (C) Oxazepam _____

   (D) Lorazepam _____

   (E) Clonazepam _____

5. A patient with hepatic dysfunction should be prescribed one of 3 benzodiazepines. Name them:

Behavioral Medicine and Ethics

6. Describe social anxiety disorder.

7. Why should buspirone not be prescribed for acute anxiety?

8. What is the most common phobia?

9. List the 3 groups of symptoms seen in PTSD:

   (A) _____

   (B) _____

   (C) _____

10. The initial treatment for a 33-year-old woman with obsessive-compulsive disorder would be which of the following?

    (A) Fluoxetine

    (B) Lithium

    (C) Lorazepam

    (D) Olanzapine

    (E) Phenelzine

11. Symptoms of panic disorder generally peak in:

    (A) 3 minutes

    (B) 5 minutes

    (C) 10 minutes

    (D) 30 minutes

    (E) 1 hour

    (F) They are persistent and do not peak.

# TOPIC 9: SOMATOFORM DISORDERS

1.  Fill in the blanks in the table below with "unconscious" or "intentional."

| Differentiating Somatoform Disorders from Factitious Disorders and Malingering | | | |
|---|---|---|---|
| | Malingering | Factitious | Somatoform |
| Symptom production | | | |
| Motivation | | | |

2.  Somatization disorder is characterized by _____ somatic symptoms that cannot be explained adequately based on _____.

3.  Somatization disorders generally have _____ pain symptoms, _____ GI symptoms, _____ sexual symptom(s), and 1 _____ symptom.

4.  Conversion disorder generally occurs following _____.

5.  A patient is diagnosed with hypochondriasis. In order to make this diagnosis, the associated "fear" with this condition should be present for how long?

    (A)   2–4 weeks

    (B)   4–12 weeks

    (C)   3–6 months

    (D)   >6 months

6. Which of the following analgesics have been proven to be most effective for pain disorder?

   (A) Acetaminophen

   (B) Aspirin

   (C) Ibuprofen

   (D) Oxycodone

   (E) Analgesic therapy is ineffective in pain disorder

7. Which of the following drug classes have been shown to be most effective for body dysmorphic disorder?

   (A) Atypical antipsychotics

   (B) NSAIDs

   (C) SSRIs

   (D) Typical antipsychotics

   (E) Body dysmorphic disorder is unresponsive to drug therapy

8. What is the primary difference between Munchausen's syndrome and Munchausen's syndrome by proxy?

9. What is the primary motivation in malingering?

Behavioral Medicine and Ethics

# TOPIC 10: PERSONALITY DISORDERS

1. What are the 5 basic dimensions of a personality?

(A) _____

(B) _____

(C) _____

(D) _____

(E) _____

2. It is believed that personality disorders may be differentiated by their _____ among the 5 dimensions rather than _____.

3. Fill in each personality disorder based on its "cluster."

| Personality Disorder by Cluster | | |
|---|---|---|
| **Cluster A** | **Cluster B** | **Cluster C** |
| | | |
| | | |
| | | |
| | | |

4. Match the personality disorder (PD) on the left with the correct phrase on the right.

(A) Antisocial PD          _____ Likely to end up as an abused spouse

(B) Avoidant PD          _____ Inflexible, orderly, rigid, perfectionist behavior

(C) Borderline PD          _____ Complete disregard for the rights of others

(D) Dependent PD          _____ Sense of entitlement and grandiosity

(E) Histrionic PD          _____ Defenses = projection

(F) Narcissistic PD          _____ Profound fear of rejection but desires relationships

(G) Obsessive compulsive PD          _____ Content in isolation and considered a loner

(H) Paranoid PD          _____ Associated with 'magical thinking'

(I) Schizoid PD          _____ Treated with mood stabilizers and anticonvulsants

(J) Schizotypal PD          _____ Defenses = regression, somatization, conversion and dissociation

# TOPIC 11: EATING DISORDERS

1. Persons with eating disorders tend to have a distorted _____.

2. Binging and purging is seen in patients with which of the following?

    (A)  Anorexia nervosa

    (B)  Bulimia nervosa

    (C)  Both conditions

    (D)  Neither condition

3. Low body weight is primarily seen in patients with which of the following?

    (A)  Anorexia nervosa

    (B)  Bulimia nervosa

    (C)  Both conditions

    (D)  Neither condition

4. Electrolyte disturbances are primarily seen in patients with which of the following?

    (A)  Anorexia nervosa

    (B)  Bulimia nervosa

    (C)  Both conditions

    (D)  Neither condition

5. The forced vomiting seen in patients with bulimia nervosa tends to occur with what frequency?

6. Enamel erosion is primarily seen in patients with which of the following?

    (A)  Anorexia nervosa

    (B)  Bulimia nervosa

    (C)  Both conditions

    (D)  Neither condition

## TOPIC 12: SEXUAL DISORDERS

1. What are the primary psychiatric disorders included in the differential for a sexual disorder?

   (A) _____

   (B) _____

   (C) _____

   (D) _____

   (E) _____

   (F) _____

   (G) _____

2. Match the sexual disorder on the left with the definition or association on the right:

   (A) Coprophilia   _____ Sexual focus on shoes

   (B) Dyspareunia   _____ Treatment with relaxation, Hegar dilators

   (C) Exhibitionism _____ Sexual pleasure derived from others' pain

   (D) Fetishism   _____ Combining sex and defecation

   (E) Frotteurism   _____ Desire to expose genitals to strangers

   (F) Sadism   _____ Recurrent pain before, during, or after intercourse

   (G) Vaginismus   _____ Act tends to occur in unknowing females on subways and buses

   (H) Voyeurism   _____ Sexual pleasure derived from watching others having sex

3. What is the difference between hypoactive sexual disorder and sexual aversion?

4. What are the treatments of choice for secondary male erectile disorder?

## TOPIC 13: SUBSTANCE ABUSE

1.  Alcoholism is characterized by _____ dependence and tolerance as well as symptoms of withdrawal when _____.

2.  Wernicke-Korsakoff syndrome is associated with a triad of symptoms. These symptoms are _____. This condition is treated with _____.

3.  A 23-year-old man who overdoses on morphine should be treated with which of the following?

    (A)   Buprenorphine

    (B)   Flumazenil

    (C)   Methadone

    (D)   Naloxone

4.  Benzodiazepines increase the _____ of $GABA_A$ channel opening, and barbiturates increase the _____ of $GABA_A$ channel opening.

5.  Which of the following exerts its mechanism of action by blocking the reuptake of dopamine, norepinephrine, and serotonin?

    (A)   Cocaine

    (B)   Lorazepam

    (C)   Methylphenidate

    (D)   Mescaline

    (E)   Phencyclidine

6.  What are the 6 basic stages of change in overcoming alcohol/drug addiction?

    (A) _____

    (B) _____

    (C) _____

    (D) _____

    (E) _____

    (F) _____

7.  Psychotherapy, drug counseling, and a 12-step program are likely to occur in which stage of overcoming alcohol/drug addiction?

    (A) Action

    (B) Contemplation

    (C) Determination

    (D) Maintenance

    (E) Pre-contemplation

    (F) Relapse

Behavioral Medicine and Ethics

# TOPIC 14: ETHICS

1. The ethical principles followed by physicians:

    (A)  Are the same throughout the United States

    (B)  Depend on the values of each individual physician

    (C)  Vary depending on the health system in which the physician is practicing

    (D)  Vary from state to state

2. The core ethical principle of "do no harm" is best described as which of the following?

    (A)  Beneficence

    (B)  Justice

    (C)  Nonmaleficence

    (D)  Patient autonomy

3. The ethical principle of justice can best be described as:



4. If a competent patient decides to go against the recommendations of the treating physician, whose preferences should always be honored?



5. Physicians have an ethical duty to act in the best interest of the patient. This ethical principle can best be described as which of the following?

    (A)  Beneficence

    (B)  Justice

    (C)  Nonmaleficence

    (D)  Patient autonomy

6. Informed consent requires that a patient _____ and _____ all the necessary information related to the procedure and/or treatment.

7. What are the 5 pieces of information that a patient must have in order for informed consent to be valid?

(A) _____

(B) _____

(C) _____

(D) _____

(E) _____

8. In informed consent, a patient must be given all the treatment alternatives, which must include the option for no _____.

9. If a patient gives a written informed consent for a procedure, how can this consent be revoked?


10. Can a patient give informed consent verbally? _____


11. Informed consent is a discussion of information where the patient _____ agrees to the care plan and must be free of _____.


12. What are the 4 exceptions to informed consent?

(A) _____

(B) _____

(C) _____

(D) _____


13. Children under the age of _____ are considered minors and legally _____.


14. Does pregnancy or giving birth in most cases emancipate a minor? _____

Behavioral Medicine and Ethics

15. Parental or guardian consent must be obtained unless the minor is _____. What are the 3 most common exceptions?

    (A) _____

    (B) _____

    (C) _____

16. Parental consent is not required for minors in which 5 situations?

    (A) _____

    (B) _____

    (C) _____

    (D) _____

    (E) _____

17. Regarding patient confidentiality, with whom is a physician permitted to discuss a patient's health-related issues without receiving patient permission?

    (A) Health care professional directly related to the care of the patient

    (B) Any physician

    (C) Patient's family

    (D) None of the above; patient must give permission

18. Is obtaining a consultation from another physician without patient permission a breach of patient confidentiality? _____

19. If a physician receives a court subpoena, what should he do?

20. What is the Tarasoff court decision?

21. Which of the following are exceptions to patient confidentiality?

    (A)   Child abuse

    (B)   Impaired automobile drivers

    (C)   Patient is a threat to oneself or others

    (D)   All of the above are correct

22. If a patient is a threat to others, the physician _____ patient confidentiality.

23. A 23-year-old man is distraught about his girlfriend having an affair. He tells the physician that he is going to kill his girlfriend and her lover. The physician calls and leaves a message on the girlfriend's cell phone. Did the physician sufficiently warn and protect the patient? _____ Explain your answer.

24. A physician must determine if the patient is _____ and _____ competent to make _____.

25. A 78-year-old man is about to undergo a surgical procedure. The patient's wife asks the physician to not tell the patient about the odds of success since she is worried that it will upset him. What should the physician do?

    (A)   Tell the spouse that she/he will provide only the best case scenario to the husband.

    (B)   Tell the spouse that she/he will not discuss the odds of success with the patient.

    (C)   Tell the spouse that she/he needs to discuss all aspects of the procedure with the patient, including the odds of success.

26. What must occur for a surrogate to make a healthcare-related decision for a patient?

    (A)   _____

    (B)   _____

    (C)   _____

Behavioral Medicine and Ethics

27. Who is given first priority as a surrogate decision-maker?

    (A)   Adult children

    (B)   Adult siblings

    (C)   Parent

    (D)   Spouse

28. If a Health Care Power of Attorney (HCPOA) determines that a patient should not receive medi-cal treatment for a condition that arose after the patient becomes incapacitated and the patient's spouse (who is not the HCPOA) wants the medical treatment administered, the physician should

    _____.

29. A physician accused of malpractice could face which of the following?

    (A)   Civil lawsuit

    (B)   Criminal charges

    (C)   Both A and B

30. What are the 4 components of malpractice?

    (A)   _____

    (B)   _____

    (C)   _____

    (D)   _____

31. What is the most common cause of a lawsuit? _____

32. Competence is a:

    (A)   Legal issue

    (B)   Medical issue

    (C)   Both A and B

33. When surrogates make decisions for a patient, physicians should base their decisions using the "best interests standard, subjective standard, and substituted judgment" in which order?

34. A 56-year-old man is deemed brain dead following a motor vehicle accident. The physician determines that there are no more treatment options but the family insists on further treatment. What should the physician do?

35. A mentally competent quadriplegic patient asks the physician to remove his feeding tube. What should the physician do?

36. Immediately prior to a necessary surgical procedure, a physician learns that the patient does not have healthcare insurance. What should the physician do?

37. A 14-year-old girl comes to the physician requesting birth control. From whom should the physician obtain consent?

38. A 12-year-old boy is in need of a life-saving surgical procedure following an accidental gunshot wound to the chest; however, the boy's parents indicate they do not want their son to have the surgery due to religious beliefs. What should the physician do?

39. A 12-year-old boy needs to have his left arm set and placed in a cast following a bicycle accident; however, the boy's parents indicate they do not want their son to undergo the procedure or have a cast on his arm due to religious beliefs. What should the physician do?

40. A mentally ill patient is committed to the hospital. Which of the following statements is true?

    (A) Patient can choose the treatments he wants to receive

    (B) Patient can leave when he wants

    (C) Patient can refuse treatment

    (D) All of the above

# Organ Systems

# Part II

# NEUROSCIENCE

## TOPIC 1: DEVELOPMENT OF THE NERVOUS SYSTEM AND ASSOCIATED PATHOLOGIES

1.  What event in embryogenesis must occur just prior to neurulation?

2.  What germ layer forms the cellular elements of both the CNS and PNS?

3.  What mesoderm structure induces the formation of the neural plate?

4.  What part of the neural tube closes first? On what day?

5.  What part of the neural tube closes second? On what day?

6.  What part of the neural tube closes third and last? On what day?

7. What functional type of neurons develop in the alar plate? Basal plate?

8. What defect results if the rostral neuropore fails to close? If the caudal neuropore fails to close?

9. Name two proteins that will be elevated in an amniocentesis if the fetus has either neural tube defect? _____

10. Which neural tube defect may also result in polyhydramnios? _____

11. Name the postnatal derivatives of the neural tube and the neural canal remnant that each contains.

| Secondary Brain Vesicle | Postnatal Derivative | Neural Canal Remnant Inside? |
|---|---|---|
| Telencephalon (name 2) | | |
| Diencephalon (name 4) | | |
| Mesencephalon | | |
| Metencephalon | | |
| Myelencephalon | | |
| Spinal cord | | |

12. Match the defect with the description.

Choices:

- Anencephaly
- Spina bifida occulta
- Dandy Walker syndrome
- Myeloschisis

- Arnold Chiari type I
- Arnold Chiari type II
- Holoprosencephaly
- Meningomyelocele

| Cause or Feature of Defect | Name of Defect |
| --- | --- |
| Incomplete separation of hemispheres; Single telencephalic ventricle | |
| Rostral neuropore fails to close | |
| Associated with trisomy 13 (Patau syndrome) | |
| Meninges line a lumbar cyst that contains the spinal cord | |
| Mildest and asymptomatic form of spina bifida | |
| Downward herniation of cerebellar vermis | |
| Failure of 4th ventricle foramina to open | |
| Associated with meningomyelocele and lower limb weakness | |
| Most severe form of spina bifida | |
| Elevated levels of AFP and AChE in amniocentesis; polyhydramnios | |
| Tuft of hair present over area with missing spinous processes | |

Neuroscience

# TOPIC 2: CYTOLOGY OF THE NERVOUS SYSTEM AND ASSOCIATED PATHOLOGIES

1. Which part of a neuron lacks Nissl substance? _____

2. Which elements of the neural cytoskeleton form neurofibrillary tangles in Alzheimer's disease?

3. Glial cell matching.

   Choices:

   - Microglia
   - Astrocytes
   - Oligodendrocytes
   - Schwann cells

| Feature | Glial Cell |
|---|---|
| Forms a single segment of myelin for a single axon | |
| Target of HIV-1 in the CNS | |
| Most numerous glial cell type in CNS | |
| Myelinates axons in tracts | |
| Macrophages of CNS | |
| Remove $K^+$ and glutamate from extracellular space | |
| Derived from bone marrow monocytes | |

4. What ATPase is necessary for anterograde axonal transport?
   For retrograde axonal transport?

5. Match the following conditions to a feature or cause:

Choices:

- Polio virus
- Rabies virus
- Tetanus toxin
- Herpes labialis (HSV-1)

- Herpes genitalis (HSV-2)
- Varicella zoster (chicken pox)
- Diabetic neuropathy

| Feature | Condition |
|---|---|
| Affects Renshaw cells in spinal cord; muscle spasms | |
| Lies dormant in Trigeminal and dorsal root ganglia; causes Shingles | |
| Lies dormant in sacral ganglia | |
| Lies dormant in Trigeminal ganglia only | |
| Causes symmetrical loss of pain and Temperature in hands and feet | |

6.  Match the feature with the appropriate demyelinating condition.

    Choices:

    - Multiple sclerosis
    - Guillain-Barré
    - Central pontine myelinosis
    - Progressive multifocal leukoencephalopathy

    - Disseminated encephalomyelinitis
    - Metachromatic leukodystrophy
    - Charcot-Marie-Tooth disease
    - Krabbe disease

| Feature | Condition |
|---|---|
| Deficient beta-galactosidase; presence of globoid cells | |
| Common inherited neurologic sensorimotor disorder; gene mutation affects neuronal proteins; pes cavus | |
| Sulfatase A deficiency; affects both PNS and CNS myelin | |
| Precipitated by *Campylobacter jejuni*; symmetrical ascending weakness, at risk for respiratory failure. | |
| Overaggressive treatment for hyponatremia; causes "locked in" syndrome | |
| CNS demyelination with no symmetry of sensory and motor deficits; optic neuritis | |
| Symptoms similar to MS; autoimmune destruction of CNS myelin | |

7.  What are the differences between the functions of an ependymal cell versus a tanycyte?

8.  List the 3 most common primary brain tumors.

9.  Which axons have the capacity to regenerate if cut? What is their rate of regeneration?

## TOPIC 3: AUTONOMIC NERVOUS SYSTEM ORGANIZATION

1.  Match a feature with a subdivision of the ANS.

    Choices:

    - Sympathetic
    - Parasympathetic
    - Both

| Feature | ANS Choice |
|---|---|
| Preganglionic neurons are cholinergic | |
| Postganglionic neurons are derived from neural crest | |
| Target tissues contain muscarinic receptors | |
| Has ganglia in the form of chromaffin cells | |
| Postganglionic neurons utilize norepinephrine as a neurotransmitter | |
| Has preganglionic cell bodies in sacral spinal cord | |
| Postganglionic neurons utilize ACh as a neurotransmitter | |
| A lesion of this system causes Horner's syndrome | |

## TOPIC 4: THE VENTRICULAR SYSTEM AND ASSOCIATED PATHOLOGIES

1. How much CSF does the choroid plexus produce per day? _____

2. How much space is in the ventricles and the subarachnoid space? _____

3. What disease might an individual with polymorphonuclear leukocytes in the CSF have?

4. What disease might an individual with elevated protein in the CSF have? _____

5. What disease might an individual with red blood cells in the CSF have? _____

6. What is the most common cause of a non-communicating hydrocephalus?

7. What is the most common cause of a communicating hydrocephalus?

8. What are the 3 symptoms of normal pressure hydrocephalus?

9. What causes hydrocephalus ex vacuo?

10. What 2 diseases most commonly cause hydrocephalus ex vacuo?

11. Name 3 lipid soluble compounds that cross the blood–brain barrier.

12. Name 2 vitamins that are transported across the blood–brain barrier.

## TOPIC 5: THE SPINAL CORD

1.  How many pairs of spinal nerves are there? _____

2.  What is the last tissue to be pierced by a spinal tap needle before it reaches the space containing the cauda equina? _____

3.  What is the difference between a dorsal root and the dorsal horn?

4.  What is the difference between a ventral root and the ventral horn?

5.  What are the functions of the largest diameter, fastest conducting fibers of the dorsal roots?

6.  What are the functions of the smallest diameter, slowest conducting fibers of the dorsal roots?

7.  What are the functions of an alpha motor neuron?

    Of a gamma motor neuron?

8. Name 2 functionally different neurons found in the intermediate zone of spinal cord gray matter.

9. Name the 2 neurons that interact to cause a voluntary contraction of skeletal muscle.

10. Name the 2 neurons that provide efferent and afferent signals from skeletal muscle during reflex contraction of the skeletal muscle.

11. Name a tendon in the upper limb and a tendon in the lower limb that can be utilized in a muscle stretch reflex.

12. Match each feature below that is characteristic of an upper motor neuron (UMN) or a lower motor neuron (LMN).

| Feature | UMN or LMN |
|---|---|
| Cell bodies are found in motor cortex | |
| Are also known as alpha motor neurons | |
| Axons cross at pyramidal decussation | |
| All parts of this neuron are ipsilateral to the innervated muscle | |
| Form the motor limb of a muscle stretch reflex | |
| Has cell bodies in the ventral horn of the cord gray matter | |
| Has a net inhibitory effect on muscle stretch reflexes | |
| A lesion results in paralysis that is ipsilateral and at the level of the lesion | |
| A lesion results in weakness with upgoing toes | |
| A lesion may cause weakness that can be ipsilateral or contralateral and below the lesion | |
| A lesion causes suppressed reflexes | |
| Lesions may result in fasciculations and atrophy | |
| A lesion may cause a clasp knife reflex | |
| Lesions cause spastic weakness and a Babinski sign | |
| Lesions may result in decerebrate or decorticate rigidity | |

13. How many neurons are needed to convey a sensory stimulus to conscious levels of cerebral cortex?

_____

14. Where does the axon of a sensory neuron cross the midline?

15. Fill in the table below with the correct components of each system.

| Feature | Dorsal Column/Medial Lemniscal System | Anterolateral System |
|---|---|---|
| Sensory functions? | | |
| Type of dorsal roots? | | |
| Axons of dorsal roots course in what tract(s)? | | |
| Location of second neuron cell body? | | |
| Axons of second neuron cross the midline of CNS in? | | |
| Axons of second neuron course in what tract? | | |
| Axons of second neuron synapse where? | | |

16. What sensation is being tested by the Romberg test? _____

    Which system? _____

17. What is tested by a tuning fork? _____

    Which system? _____

18. Which specific tract carries vibratory sense from the lower limb through the cord? _____

19. Which specific tract carries vibratory sense from the upper limb through the cord? _____

20. Which specific tract carries pain and temperature through the cord? _____

21. What sensory information is carried by the dorsal spinocerebellar tract?

    _____

    From where? _____

22. What sensory information is carried by the cuneocerebellar tract?

    _____

    From where? _____

23. What chromosome contains a defective gene that encodes for Friedreich's ataxia?

24. List 3 deficits in an infant born with Friedreich's ataxia.

Neuroscience

25. Match a feature or symptom of a lesion with the tracts in the table below. More than one choice may be correct.

| Symptom or Feature | Fasiciculus Gracilis | Fasiciculus Cuneatus | Spiniothalamic Tract | Lissauer's Tract |
|---|---|---|---|---|
| Loss of vibratory sense from ipsilateral lower limb | | | | |
| Loss of pain and temperature from several dermatomes ipsilateral to a lesion | | | | |
| Loss of pain and temperature contralateral and below a lesion | | | | |
| Has cell bodies in the ipsilateral dorsal horn | | | | |
| Axons cross in the cord | | | | |
| Contains A-delta and C dorsal roots | | | | |
| Has neuron cell bodies in ipsilateral dorsal root ganglia (more than one answer) | | | | |

26. Identify points A–G of the spinal cord cross section below and fill in the table to describe the effects caused by a lesion at each location.

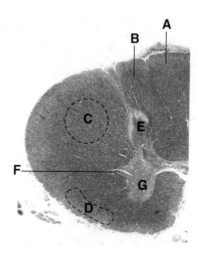

| | Identify A–G | Lesions of A–G Result In | Deficit is Ipsi- or Contralateral to Lesion |
|---|---|---|---|
| A | | | |
| B | | | |
| C | | | |
| D | | | |
| E | | | |
| F | | | |
| G | | | |

27. For each symptom or feature below, place an "X" under the associated condition. Some may be found in more than one condition.

| Symptom or Feature | Anterior Spinal Artery Occlusion | Amyotrophic Lateral Sclerosis | Poliomyelitis | Werdnig Hoffman Disease |
|---|---|---|---|---|
| Bilateral paralysis with suppressed reflexes | | | | |
| Bilateral spastic weakness in lower limbs; bilateral flaccid weakness in upper limbs | | | | |
| Bilateral spastic weakness and bilateral loss of pain and temperature | | | | |
| Bilateral flaccid weakness, hypotonia and tongue fasciculations | | | | |

28. For each symptom or feature below, place an "X" under the associated condition. Some may be found in more than one condition.

| Symptom or Feature | Brown Sequard Syndrome | Syringomyelia | Tabes dorsalis | Subacute Combined Degeneration |
|---|---|---|---|---|
| Altered vibratory sense in lower limbs, urine retention, pain, and Romberg sign | | | | |
| Ipsilateral loss of vibratory sense, ipsilateral spastic weakness, contralateral loss of pain, and temperature | | | | |
| Bilateral loss of pain and temperature initially; bilateral flaccid paralysis | | | | |
| Bilateral loss of vibratory sense, bilateral spastic weakness | | | | |

# TOPIC 6: THE BRAINSTEM

1.  Which cranial nerves arise from the midbrain? _____

2.  Which cranial nerves arise from the pons? _____

3.  Which cranial nerves arise from the medulla? _____

4.  In the table below, indicate whether a tract lesion will cause ipsilateral or contralateral signs and symptoms.

| Tract in Brainstem | Sign and Symptoms Ipsilateral and Below the Lesion | Sign and Symptoms Contralateral and Below the Lesion |
|---|---|---|
| Corticospinal tract | | |
| Medial lemniscus | | |
| Spinothalamic tract | | |
| Descending hypothalamic fibers | | |
| Fasciculus gracilis | | |
| Fasciculus cuneatus | | |

5.  For each cranial nerve below, place an "X" under its function(s).

| Cranial Nerve | Innervates Skeletal Muscle of Myotome Origin | Innervates Smooth Muscle, Glands, or Heart | Innervates Skeletal Muscle in a Pharyngeal Arch | Conveys Touch, Pain, or Temperature | Conveys Taste | Innervates Chemo- or Baro-receptors |
|---|---|---|---|---|---|---|
| Oculomotor | | | | | | |
| Trochlear | | | | | | |
| Abducens | | | | | | |
| Hypoglossal | | | | | | |
| Trigeminal | | | | | | |
| Facial | | | | | | |
| Glossopha-ryngeal | | | | | | |
| Vagus | | | | | | |
| Accessory | | | | | | |

6. For each cranial nerve below, describe its general function, how it is tested, and the sign or symptoms present if lesioned.

| Cranial Nerve | Function(s) | Test | Sign or Symptoms if Lesioned |
|---|---|---|---|
| Oculomotor | | | |
| Trochlear | | | |
| Abducens | | | |
| Trigeminal | | | |
| Facial | | | |
| Glossopharyngeal | | | |
| Vagus | | | |
| Accessory | | | |
| Optic | | | |
| Vestibulocochlear | | | |
| Olfactory | | | |

Neuroscience

7.  Label points A–K.

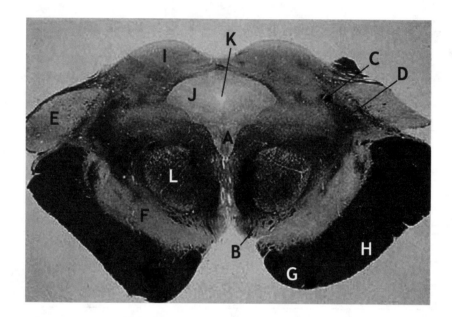

| | Structure |
|---|---|
| A | |
| B | |
| C | |
| D | |
| E | |
| F | |
| G | |
| H | |
| I | |
| J | |
| K | |

8. Label points A–H.

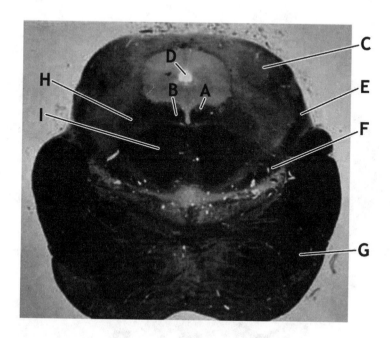

| | Structure |
|---|---|
| A | |
| B | |
| C | |
| D | |
| E | |
| F | |
| G | |
| H | |

Neuroscience

9.  Label points A–H.

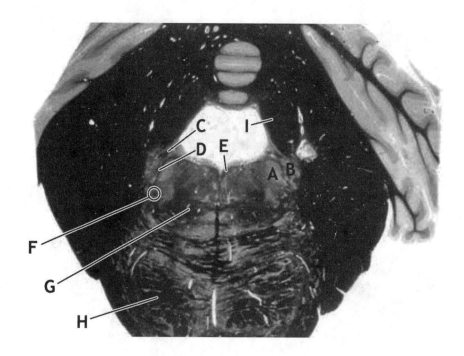

|   | Structure |
|---|-----------|
| A |           |
| B |           |
| C |           |
| D |           |
| E |           |
| F |           |
| G |           |
| H |           |

10. Label points A–K.

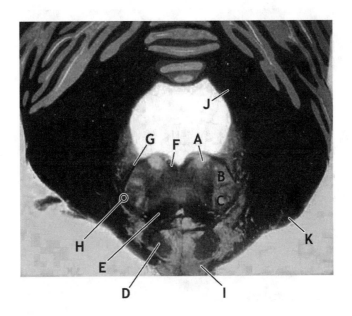

| | Structure |
|---|---|
| A | |
| B | |
| C | |
| D | |
| E | |
| F | |
| G | |
| H | |
| I | |
| J | |
| K | |

11.  Label points A–N.

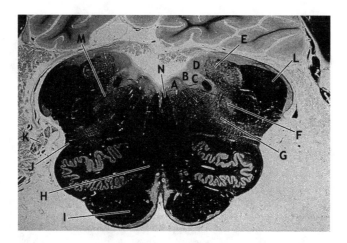

| | Structure |
|---|---|
| A | |
| B | |
| C | |
| D | |
| E | |
| F | |
| G | |
| H | |
| I | |
| J | |
| K | |
| L | |
| M | |
| N | |

12. Label points A–G.

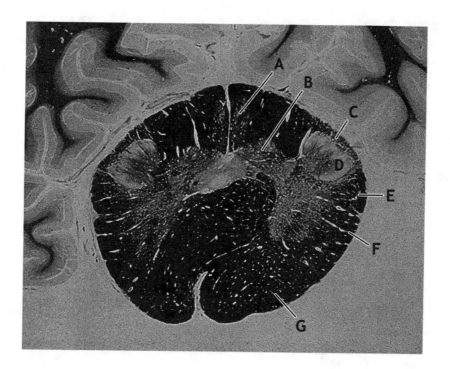

|   | Structure |
|---|-----------|
| A |           |
| B |           |
| C |           |
| D |           |
| E |           |
| F |           |
| G |           |

13. Fill in the table below regarding trigeminal structures.

| Trigeminal-related Structure | Function | Lesion Results In |
|---|---|---|
| Main sensory nucleus of V | | |
| Motor nucleus of V | | |
| Spinal nucleus of V | | |
| Mesencephalic nucleus of V | | |
| Ventral posterior medial nucleus of thalamus | | |
| Trigeminal ganglion | | |

14. What is the most common deficit seen if all of the corticobulbar axons are lesioned on one side?

    _____

15. Name the three parts of the ear. _____

    Which ones are air-filled? Fluid-filled? _____

16. What specialized fluid bathes the hairs of all inner ear hair cells? _____

17. What are the frequency response characteristics of hair cells at the base of the cochlea? Apex of the cochlea?

18. Where are hair cells lost in someone who develops presbycusis? _____

19. If bone conduction of sound is better than air conduction, where is the lesion?

   _____

20. If air conduction of sound is better than bone conduction, where is the lesion?

   _____

21. What is the first site in the central auditory pathway where sound localization processing begins?

22. What does the Weber test determine?

23. What does the Rinne test determine?

24. Which vestibular system is stimulated when the head is turned horizontally to the right?

25. Which direction do the eyes move in response to head turning?

26. If there is a lesion of the right vestibular nuclei, what is the direction of the fast or corrective phase of the vestibular evoked nystagmus?

27. What does COWS stand for with regard to caloric testing?

28. For each finding listed below, indicate where the lesion would be located.

| Ocular System Lesions; Feature | Frontal Eye Field | PPRF | MLF | CN III | CN IV |
|---|---|---|---|---|---|
| Cannot look away from side of lesion; right upper limb and right lower face weakness | | | | | |
| Cannot look toward side of lesion; complete facial weakness | | | | | |
| Cannot adduct an eye during attempted horizontal gaze; convergence is intact | | | | | |
| Cannot adduct an eye under any conditions | | | | | |
| Cannot abduct an eye | | | | | |
| Dilated pupil, ptosis, external strabismus | | | | | |
| Internal strabismus | | | | | |

29. For each feature, indicate an associated syndrome. Each can be associated with more than one syndrome.

| Features | Lateral Medullary Syndrome | Medial Medullary Syndrome | Lateral Pontine Syndrome | Medial Pontine Syndrome | Medial Midbrain Syndrome |
|---|---|---|---|---|---|
| Spastic weakness in contralateral limbs | | | | | |
| Loss of vibratory sense in contralateral body and limbs | | | | | |
| Loss of pain and temperature in contralateral body and limbs | | | | | |
| Ptosis, miosis, anhydrosis | | | | | |
| Cranial nerve(s) affected (name them) | | | | | |
| Analgesia of ipsilateral face | | | | | |
| Nystagmus | | | | | |
| Sensorineural hearing loss | | | | | |
| Blocked artery cause | | | | | |

## TOPIC 7: THE CEREBELLUM, BASAL GANGLIA, AND MOVEMENT DISORDERS

1. Compare and contrast the functions of the cerebellum and basal ganglia.

| Feature | Basal Ganglia | Cerebellum |
|---|---|---|
| Initiates movement | | |
| Coordinates movement | | |
| Utilizes GABA and glutamate as neurotransmitters | | |
| Lesions cause tremor at rest | | |
| Lesions cause tremor with movement | | |
| Major output projects to VA/VL nuclei of thalamus | | |
| Modulates activity of upper motor neurons | | |

2. Compare and contrast the functions of the cerebellar hemisphere and vermis.

| Feature | Cerebellar Hemisphere | Cerebellar Vermis |
|---|---|---|
| Controls axial and proximal limb muscles | | |
| Control distal muscles | | |
| Lesions cause dysmetria | | |
| Lesions cause truncal ataxia | | |
| Lesions cause dysdiadochokinesis | | |
| Lesions cause gait ataxia | | |
| Deficits are ipsilateral to lesion side | | |

3. Compare and contrast the functions of the direct and indirect basal ganglia pathways.

| Feature | Direct Basal Ganglia Pathway | Indirect Basal Ganglia Pathway |
|---|---|---|
| Initiates desired movement | | |
| Suppresses unwanted movement | | |
| Uses two GABA neurons to disinhibit VA/VL thalamus | | |
| Uses 2 GABA neurons to disinhibit the subthalamic nucleus | | |
| Driven by excitation from cortex | | |
| Functions enhanced by dopamine | | |
| Functions enhanced by acetylcholine | | |
| Pathway begins with GABA neurons in the striatum | | |

Neuroscience

4. Compare and contrast the following conditions by placing an "X" next to each associated feature.

| Features | Parkinson Disease | Huntington's Disease | Wilson's Disease | Hemiballismus |
|---|---|---|---|---|
| Loss of dopamine output from substantia nigra, pars compacta | | | | |
| Atrophy of the caudate nucleus | | | | |
| Autosomal dominance; unstable nucleotide repeat | | | | |
| Kayser-Fleischer ring is pathognomonic | | | | |
| Bradykinesia, masked facial expression, shuffling gait, pill rolling tremor | | | | |
| Chorea and athetosis present | | | | |
| Asterixis; wing beating tremor | | | | |
| Caused by lacunar stroke of subthalamic nucleus | | | | |
| May be caused by MPTP by-product of heroin synthesis | | | | |
| Lewy bodies are pathognomonic | | | | |
| Results in involuntary flinging movements contralateral to lesion side | | | | |

5. Label points A–I.

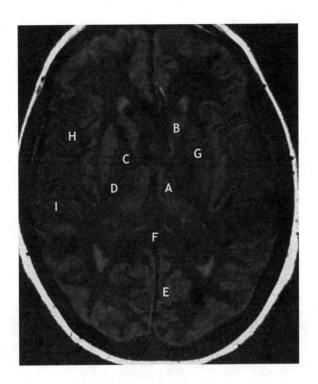

| | Structure |
|---|---|
| A | |
| B | |
| C | |
| D | |
| E | |
| F | |
| G | |
| H | |
| I | |

Neuroscience

# TOPIC 8: THE EYE AND VISUAL PATHWAYS

1. Name the nerves and nuclei that form the circuit of the pupillary light reflex pathway.

2. What disease condition will result in a "blue sclera"?

3. What is the cause of open angle versus closed angle glaucoma?

4. Complete the autonomic innervation of the eye in the table below.

| Structure | Predominant Receptor | Receptor Innervation | Receptor Activation Causes | Receptor Blockage Causes |
|---|---|---|---|---|
| Pupillary sphincter | M3 | CN III (ciliary ganglion) | | Mydriasis |
| Pupillary dilator | | Postgangionic sympathetics (SCG) | Dilation | Miosis |
| | | CN III (ciliary ganglion) | Contraction; lens gets rounder | Relaxation; lens gets flatter |
| Ciliary muscle | β-adrenergic | CN III (ciliary ganglion) | Increased secretion | Decreased secretion of aqueous humor |

5. For each effect, place an "X" under the responsible class of drug.

| Effects of Glaucoma Drugs | Beta-blockers (Timolol) | Cholinomimetics | Prostaglandin Analogue (Latanoprost) |
|---|---|---|---|
| Decrease synthesis of aqueous humor | | | |
| Increase outflow of aqueous humor | | | |

6. Review the common diseases of the eye in the table below.

| Structure | Myopia | Hyperopia | Astigmatism | Presbyopia | Cataracts |
|---|---|---|---|---|---|
| Eyeball too long; image focuses in front of retina | | | | | |
| Irregular curvature of cornea | | | | | |
| Loss of lens elasticity | | | | | |
| Eyeball too short; image focuses in back of retina | | | | | |
| Progressive opacification of lens | | | | | |

Neuroscience

7.  Match the findings with their cause by placing an "X" in the appropriate cell.

| Feature | Argyll Robertson Pupil | Adie Pupil | Mydriasis with Ptosis | Miosis with Ptosis, Dry Face | Marcus Gunn Pupil |
|---|---|---|---|---|---|
| Caused by mass effect and uncal herniation | | | | | |
| Caused by degeneration of a ciliary ganglion | | | | | |
| Caused by demyelination of pretectal area | | | | | |
| Caused by a lesion of descending hypothalamic axons | | | | | |
| Caused by berry aneurysm compression | | | | | |
| Demonstrated by swinging flashlight test | | | | | |
| Seen with multiple sclerosis | | | | | |
| Both pupils constrict in the near response but less briskly in response to light | | | | | |

Neuroscience

8. Match the cause or feature with a visual field deficit in A–I.

| | |
|---|---|
| Caused by a right temporal lobe tumor | |
| Caused by a blockage of the central artery of the retina | |
| Caused by a lesion of the right optic tract | |
| Caused by a medially expanding aneurysm of the right internal carotid artery | |
| Caused by complete compression of the optic chiasm | |
| Caused by a lesion of the cuneus gyrus | |
| Seen in a patient with multiple sclerosis | |
| Caused by compression by a small craniopharyngioma | |
| Caused by a lesion to the left lingual gyrus | |
| Caused by a lesion to Meyer's loop on the right | |
| Caused by a complete blockage of the posterior cerebral artery (2 answers) | |

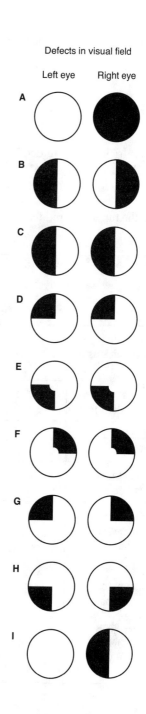

Defects in visual field

Left eye    Right eye

Neuroscience

## TOPIC 9: THE DIENCEPHALON

9.  Name the 4 parts of the diencephalon.

10. What ventricle is surrounded by the diencephalon? _____

11. Match the functions and features to the thalamic nuclei below.

| Function/ Feature | Ventral Postero-lateral | Ventral Postero-medial | Lateral Genicu-late | Medial Genicu-late | Ventral Anterior/ Ventral Lateral | Dorso-medial |
|---|---|---|---|---|---|---|
| Relays taste from solitary nucleus to cortex | | | | | | |
| Gives rise to the visual radiations | | | | | | |
| Projects to the temporal lobe | | | | | | |
| Projects to motor cortex | | | | | | |
| Degenerates in thiamine-deficient alcoholics | | | | | | |
| Relays body and limb somatosen-sory information to cortex | | | | | | |
| Relays facial sensation to cortex | | | | | | |

12. Match the function or feature to the hypothalamic nuclei below.

| Function/ Feature | Mammillary | Suprachi-asmatic | Supraoptic/ Paraventricular | Arcuate | Ventromedial |
|---|---|---|---|---|---|
| Receives direct retinal input for circadian rhythm | | | | | |
| Secretes releasing and inhibiting factors | | | | | |
| Releases ADH into posterior pituitary | | | | | |
| A satiety center | | | | | |
| Neurons degenerate here in thiamine-deficient alcoholics | | | | | |
| Influences melatonin release by the pineal | | | | | |

Neuroscience

# TOPIC 10: THE CEREBRAL CORTEX

1.  What two lobes are separated by the central sulcus?

2.  What lies above and below the lateral fissure?

3.  What part of the motor homunculus is represented on the lateral aspect of the precentral gyrus?

4.  What is the dual arterial blood supply of the motor and the sensory homunculus?

5.  What is the difference between allocortex and neocortex?

6.  Match the feature with the correct intracranial bleed.

| Features of Intracranial Bleeds | Intraventricular | Epidural | Subdural | Subarachnoid |
|---|---|---|---|---|
| Caused by tears in middle meningeal artery | | | | |
| Lucid interval, uncal herniation | | | | |
| Bleeding berry aneurysm, thunderclap headache, nuchal rigidity | | | | |
| Premature infant, bleeding in germinal matrix | | | | |
| Head trauma lacerates cerebral veins that drain into dural sinuses; drowsiness and dementia | | | | |
| Associated with Marfan syndrome, Ehlers-Danlos syndrome, and APKD | | | | |

7. In the table below, match the lobe with the feature of a lesion.

| Feature | Frontal Lobe | Parietal Lobe | Temporal Lobe | Occipital Lobe |
|---|---|---|---|---|
| Unilateral neglect (right side) | | | | |
| Spastic weakness | | | | |
| Bilateral hearing loss | | | | |
| Homonymous hemianopsia with macular sparing | | | | |
| Facial numbness | | | | |
| Loss of horizontal conjugate gaze | | | | |
| Achromatopsia and prosopagnosia | | | | |
| Loss of the ability to track moving objects | | | | |

8. Match the feature with the condition using an "X."

| Feature | Motor Aphasia | Sensory Aphasia | Gerstmann Syndrome | Conduction Aphasia |
|---|---|---|---|---|
| Alexia and agraphia, finger agnosia, dyscalculia | | | | |
| Speech reduced to single syllable words, frustrated by deficit | | | | |
| Oral comprehension deficit, bilateral hearing loss, unaware of deficit | | | | |
| Normal but paraphasic speech, comprehension intact, cannot name objects, frustrated by deficit | | | | |

9. Name 2 locations of lesions that cause a disconnect syndrome.

10. What tracts pass through the posterior limb of the internal capsule?

11. What tract passes through the genu of the internal capsule?

12. Match each feature with the white matter lesion site.

| Feature | Arcuate Fasciculus | Genu of Internal Capsule | Posterior Limb of Internal Capsule | Corpus Callosum |
|---|---|---|---|---|
| Contralateral lower face weakness; no other CN deficits | | | | |
| Contralateral limb and trunk anesthesia | | | | |
| Cannot move left limb in response to command; no weakness | | | | |
| Normal but paraphasic speech, comprehension intact, cannot name objects, frustrated by deficit | | | | |
| Cannot read but can write; other language functions intact | | | | |

13. Match each feature with the limbic system lesions.

| Sign, Symptom or Feature | Alzheimer's Disease | Kluver-Bucy Syndrome | Wernicke-Korsakoff Syndrome |
|---|---|---|---|
| Lesions result in one becoming placid with loss of sexual preference | | | |
| Lesions result in progressive anterograde amnesia for events in time | | | |
| Lesions result in retrograde amnesia with confabulations | | | |
| Lesions caused by thiamine deficiency | | | |
| Associated with gait ataxia and diplopia | | | |

14. Name a cortical neurotransmitter that is reduced in Alzheimer's dementia. _____

15. What subcortical neuronal system projects directly to cortex without a thalamic relay?

Neuroscience

## TOPIC 11: CNS DISORDERS

1.  With respect to the affected areas in the brain, what are the differences between Pick's disease and Alzheimer's disease?

2.  Match the disease on the left with the histological-gross findings on the right.

    (A) Alzheimer's disease      _____ Kayser-Fleischer rings

    (B) Creutzfeldt-Jakob disease      _____ Neurofibrillary tangles

    (C) Lewy body dementia      _____ Spongiform cortex

    (D) Pick's disease      _____ Spherical tau protein aggregates

    (E) Wilson's disease      _____ Alpha-synuclein defect

         _____ Senile plaques

         _____ $PrP^C \rightarrow PrP^{SC}$ sheet

         _____ Frontotemporal atrophy

3.  What are the 4 A's of complex seizures?

4.  Match the generalized seizure disorder on the left with the appropriate characteristic on the right.

    (A) Absence      _____ Epileptiform activity or focal, localizing activity on EEG

    (B) Myoclonic      _____ Seizure activity lasting 30 minutes

    (C) Status epilepticus      _____ Single or multiple myoclonic jerks

    (D) Tonic-clonic      _____ Generalized 3 Hz spike-and-wave on EEG

         _____ Treated with ethosuximide

         _____ Grand mal seizure

         _____ Petite mal seizure

5. Fill in the blanks in the table below for commonly used anticonvulsants.

| Drug | Mechanism | Notes |
|------|-----------|-------|
| Benzodiazepines | | Sedation, dependence, tolerance |
| | Blocks axonal $Na^+$ channels in inactivated state | CNS depression, diplopia, ataxia, osteomalacia, megaloblastic and aplastic anemia, exfoliative dermatitis, dilutional hypernatremia (increased ADH secretion), cytochrome P450 inducer, hepatotoxicity, teratogenic |
| Ethosuximide | | GI distress, headache, lethargy, hematotoxicity, Stevens-Johnson syndrome |
| Felbamate | | |
| | GABA analogue | Sedation, ataxia |
| Lamotrigine | Blocks $Na^+$ channels and glutamate receptors | |
| Phenobarbital | | Induction of cytochrome P450, sedation, dependence, tolerance |
| | | Gingival hyperplasia, hirsutism, sedation, anemia, nystagmus, diplopia, ataxia, teratogenic (fetal hydantoin syndrome), P450 induction, zero-order kinetics |
| | Believed to inhibit voltage-dependent sodium channels and enhance GABA activity | Sedation, dizziness, ataxia, anomia, renal stones, weight loss |
| Valproic acid | | GI distress, hepatotoxic (rare but can be fatal), inhibits drug metabolism, neural tube defects |

6. Describe the clinical presentation for a patient with a cluster headache.

7. A patient with a classic migraine takes a medication that activates vascular serotonin 5-HT1 receptors. What medication did the patient receive?

   (A) Ergotamine

   (B) Fluoxetine

   (C) Propranolol

   (D) Sumatriptan

   (E) Verapamil

8. Cluster headaches can be differentiated from trigeminal neuralgia based on _____.

9. A patient is diagnosed with an autosomal dominant condition that is associated with the development of hamartomatous lesions that can affect every organ as well as ash leaf spots. What is the most likely diagnosis?

   (A) Neurofibromatosis

   (B) Sturge-Weber syndrome

   (C) Tuberous sclerosis

   (D) von Hippel-Lindau disease

10. Nevus flammeus in Sturge-Weber syndrome is generally present along a distribution of what cranial nerve?

    (A) I

    (B) II

    (C) III

    (D) IV

    (E) V

11. The etiology of neurofibromatosis type 1 can best be described as _____.

12. A patient is diagnosed with neurofibromatosis type 1. Which of the following would be an expected finding in this patient?

    (A) Ash leaf spots

    (B) Café-au-lait spots

    (C) Cavernous hemangiomas in skin, mucosa and organs

    (D) Cutaneous angiofibroma

    (E) Nevus flammeus

13. Von Hippel-Lindau disease is an autosomal _____ disorder caused by a mutation of

    _____.

14. A patient is diagnosed with a prolactinoma. Recommended treatment options include

    _____.

15. A patient with a somatotrope adenoma would most likely have which of the following features?

    (A) Amenorrhea

    (B) Galactorrhea

    (C) Short stature

    (D) Tall stature

16. Which of the following would be expected in a patient with hemangioblastoma?

    (A) Agranulocytosis

    (B) Leukocytosis

    (C) Pancytopenia

    (D) Polycythemia

Neuroscience

17. Pathologic examination of a patient's tumor shows blue, small, round cells with Homer-Wright pseudorosettes. Which of the following is the most likely diagnosis?

    (A) Craniopharyngioma

    (B) Glioblastoma multiforme

    (C) Medulloblastoma

    (D) Meningioma

    (E) Oligodendroglioma

    (F) Pilocytic astrocytoma (grade 1)

    (G) Schwannoma

18. During a procedure, a patient is administered a medication that causes the following: serum potassium 6.1 mEq/L, hypercarbia with acidosis, muscle rigidity, and temperature of 40°C (104°F). The most likely diagnosis is _____. The condition is most commonly caused by _____. It is treated with _____.

19. Following a procedure where a 48-year-old male was administered a general anesthetic, his hepatic enzymes become elevated. Which of the following agents was most likely administered to this patient?

    (A) Enflurane

    (B) Desflurane

    (C) Halothane

    (D) Isoflurane

    (E) Methoxyflurane

    (F) Nitrous Oxide

20. Would the effects of succinylcholine be reversed with neostigmine? _____ Why or why not?

# CHAPTER 2

# MUSCULOSKELETAL AND CONNECTIVE TISSUE

## TOPIC 1: DERMATOLOGY

1. Complete the following table.

| Feature | Stratum Basale | Stratum Spinosum | Stratum Granulosum | Stratum Corneum | Stratum Lucidum |
|---|---|---|---|---|---|
| Contains stem cells | | | | | |
| Cells linked by desmosomes | | | | | |
| Attached to underlying basement membrane | | | | | |
| Contains melanocytes | | | | | |
| Found only in "thick" skin | | | | | |

2. Complete the following table.

| Feature | Zonula Occludens | Zonula Adherens | Desmosome | Gap Junction | Hemi-Desmosome |
|---|---|---|---|---|---|
| Polarizes an epithelium | | | | | |
| Contains connexons | | | | | |
| Utilizes cadherins as adhesive molecules | | | | | |
| Linked to intracellular actin | | | | | |
| Utilizes claudins as adhesive molecules | | | | | |
| Utilizes desmoplakin to link to intermediate filaments | | | | | |
| Attaches the cell to the underlying ECM | | | | | |
| Utilizes integrin adhesive molecules | | | | | |
| Disrupted in pemphigus vulgaris | | | | | |
| Disrupted in bullous pemphigoid | | | | | |
| Blocks paracellular diffusion | | | | | |
| Permits cell-to-cell communication | | | | | |

3. Describe the size and appearance of a macule and a patch, and state which is bigger.

4. Describe the size and appearance of a plaque and a papule, and state which is bigger.

5. What is the difference between a vesicle and a wheal?

6. A clear fluid containing a raised skin lesion larger than 1 cm is called _____.

7. An area of scar that becomes markedly hypertrophied is called _____.

8. Complete the following table.

| Finding | Example of Condition |
|---|---|
| Crust | |
| Hyperkeratosis | |
| Parakeratosis | |
| Acantholysis | |

9. Hyperkeratosis with retention of nuclei in stratum corneum is referred to as _____.

10. Separation of the epidermal cells from one another is referred to as _____.

11. Name 2 skin diseases that can be caused by human papillomavirus.

12. A nevus that contains atypical cells is called _____.

13. What is the mechanism of formation of hives?

14. Acanthosis with parakeratotic scaling, increased thickness of the stratum spinosum, and decreased thickness of the stratum granulosum are characteristic of which condition?

15. What occurs when a psoriatic lesion is scraped?

16. Which type of albinism is associated with an increased risk of cancer?

17. How does the extent of involvement of skin and subcutaneous tissues differ between cellulitis and necrotizing fasciitis?

18. The target of autoantibodies in pemphigus vulgaris is _____.

19. The target of autoantibodies in bullous pemphigoid is _____.

20. Dermatitis herpetiformis is associated with what disease?

21. Name a very severe eruption similar to erythema multiforme.

22. Acanthosis nigricans is associated with what systemic conditions?

23. The painful nodules on the shins of patients with sarcoidosis are called _____.

24. What lesion commonly precedes development of a squamous cell carcinoma?

25. The whorled, densely eosinophilic protein and large cells in squamous cell carcinoma are called

_____.

26. A pearly papule lesion with rolled edges located on the upper face is likely to be

_____.

27. A large, dark, multicolored skin lesion with irregular borders is likely to be

    _____.

28. What marker can be used to assess tumor recurrence after resection of a melanoma?

## TOPIC 2: ANATOMY AND PHYSIOLOGY OF MUSCLES AND LIGAMENTS

1. Name the calcium channel in the T tubule membrane.

2. Name the calcium channel in the sarcoplasmic reticulum membrane.

3. Do skeletal muscle cells have one or more than one nucleus? Where is the nucleus situated in the cell?

4. Complete the following table.

| Feature | H Zone | A Band | I Band | Z Line |
|---|---|---|---|---|
| Changes length during sarcomere shortening | | | | |
| Marks the end of each sarcomere | | | | |
| Band is found in 2 adjacent sarcomeres | | | | |
| Band marks the length of the myosin filaments | | | | |
| Band marks the center of the sarcomere | | | | |
| Band does not change length when the sarcomere shortens | | | | |

Musculoskeletal and Connective Tissue

5. Name the 4 key proteins involved in the physiology of skeletal muscle and briefly describe their functions.

6. Sketch the sequence of events that occurs in the neuromuscular junction when an action potential is evoked in an alpha-motor neuron.

7. The _____ receptor is located on T tubules. It is a

_____ $Ca^{2+}$ channel that _____ the ryanodine receptor,

which is the _____ on the sarcoplasmic reticulum (SR).

8. Sketch the sequence of events that occurs when an action potential travels down the T-tubule.

9. Describe the 2 key roles that ATP plays with respect to the power stroke.

10. What happens if a striated muscle cell is depleted of ATP?

11. For the table below, place up or down arrows before each item to distinguish the important differences between slow twitch and fast twitch muscle fibers. Complete the final row to indicate what each is "best suited" for functionally.

| Slow Twitch (Type I) | Fast Twitch (Type II) |
| --- | --- |
| Myosin ATPase activity | Myosin ATPase activity |
| Aerobic capacity | Aerobic capacity |
| Mitochondrial content | Mitochondrial content |
| Myoglobin | Myoglobin |
| Best for | Best for |

12. What is meant by fiber grouping, and when does it typically occur?

13. Sketch the sequence of events that occurs to produce contraction of smooth muscle.

14. Indicate what happens in smooth muscle on a cellular level if the cytosolic concentration of IP3, cAMP, or cGMP increases.

15. Name 3 functions of the thenar and hypothenar eminence.

Musculoskeletal and Connective Tissue

16. What nerves innervate muscles in the thenar and hypothenar eminence?

17. What are the functional differences between the dorsal and palmar interosseous muscles?

18. What functions do lumbrical muscles have at the MP joints? IP joints?

19. What two nerves innervate lumbricals?

20. What condition occurs if lumbricals are denervated?

21. The 4 SITS (rotator cuff) muscles are:

22. Which SITS muscle is not a rotator?

23. Which SITS muscle abducts to 15 degrees?

24. Which SITS muscle takes over abduction above 15 degrees?

25. Which SITS muscles laterally rotate the arm at the shoulder?

26. Which SITS muscle medially rotates the arm at the shoulder?

27. Complete the following table.

| Feature | Anterior Cruciate Ligament | Posterior Cruciate Ligament | Medial Collateral Ligament | Lateral Collateral Ligament | Medial Meniscus | Lateral Meniscus |
|---|---|---|---|---|---|---|
| Attaches to anterior tibial plateau | | | | | | |
| Attaches to medial femoral condyle | | | | | | |
| Tested by passive adduction of leg | | | | | | |
| Tested while pulling the leg anteriorly while stabilizing the femur | | | | | | |
| Injury causes a posterior drawer sign | | | | | | |
| Attaches to the fibula | | | | | | |
| Three injured components of the "unhappy triad" | | | | | | |

28. What elbow ligament is stretched in "golfer's elbow"?

29. What elbow ligament is stretched in "tennis elbow"?

# TOPIC 3: INNERVATION OF THE EXTREMITIES

1.  Label the main brachial plexus nerves.

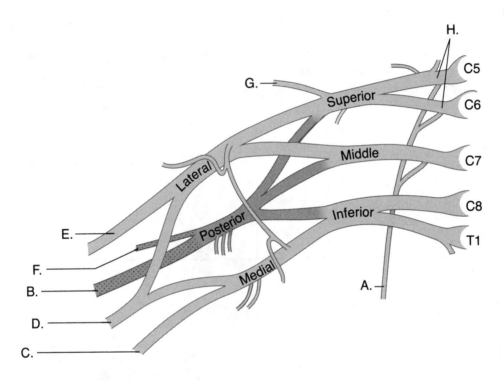

| | Identify |
|---|---|
| A | |
| B | |
| C | |
| D | |
| E | |
| F | |
| G | |
| H | |

2. What ventral rami form the brachial plexus roots?

3. What cord segments are in the upper and lower trunks?

4. What cord segments are in the musculocutaneous nerve and the axillary nerve?

5. What cord segments are in the ulnar nerve?

6. Shoulder dystocia injures what part of the plexus?

7. Name 2 causes of lower trunk compression.

8. Complete the following table.

| Feature | Musculo-cutaneous Nerve | Median Nerve | Ulnar Nerve | Radial Nerve | Axillary Nerve |
|---|---|---|---|---|---|
| Lesioned by surgical neck humeral fracture | | | | | |
| Lesioned by spiral groove fracture of humerus | | | | | |
| Compressed by misuse of crutch | | | | | |
| Lesioned by radius subluxation | | | | | |
| Lesioned by medial epicondylar humeral fracture | | | | | |
| Lesioned by supracondylar humeral fracture | | | | | |
| Stretched by humeral dislocation | | | | | |

9. Fill in the corresponding nerve dermatomes for each anatomic area.

| | Corresponding Dermatome(s) |
|---|---|
| Axilla | |
| Medial forearm | |
| Lateral forearm | |
| Lateral palm | |
| Medial palm | |
| Lateral part of dorsum of hand | |

10. Complete the following table.

| Feature | Musculo-cutaneous Nerve | Median Nerve | Ulnar Nerve | Radial Nerve | Axillary Nerve |
|---|---|---|---|---|---|
| Cord segments in? | | | | | |
| Location of altered sensation if lesioned? | | | | | |
| Motor weakness if lesioned? | | | | | |
| Sign associated with motor deficit? | | | | | |

11. Complete the following table.

| Feature | Upper Trunk | Lower Trunk | Long Thoracic Nerve |
|---|---|---|---|
| Cord segments in? | | | |
| Location of altered sensation if lesioned? | | | |
| Motor weakness if lesioned? | | | |
| Sign associated with motor deficit? | | | |

12. Complete the following table.

| Feature | Obturator Nerve | Femoral Nerve | Tibial Nerve | Common Fibular Nerve |
|---|---|---|---|---|
| Cord segments in? | | | | |
| Location of altered sensation if lesioned? | | | | |
| Motor weakness if lesioned? | | | | |
| Sign associated with motor deficit? | | | | |

13. Complete the following table.

| Feature | Superficial Fibular Nerve | Deep Fibular Nerve | Superior Gluteal Nerve | Inferior Gluteal Nerve |
|---|---|---|---|---|
| Cord segments in? | | | | |
| Location of altered sensation if lesioned? | | | | |
| Motor weakness if lesioned? | | | | |
| Sign associated with motor deficit? | | | | |

14. What ligament is commonly torn in an inversion sprain?

15. Which other 2 bones may be fractured or avulsed by an inversion ankle sprain?

## TOPIC 4: DISORDERS OF THE BONES

1. What is the molecular defect in achondroplasia?

2. Which bone disease is characterized by decreased bone mass, particularly in older adults?

3. The decreased estrogen involved in the etiology of type 1 osteoporosis has what effect on RANK receptor expression?

4. What patient population develops type 2 osteoporosis?

5. What fractures are common among osteoporosis patients?

6. The main class of drugs used in the management of osteoporosis is the

   _____. These drugs have a common ending to their names, which is

   _____.

7. A patient started on a drug in the class mentioned in the previous question is advised to remain upright for 30 minutes following drug administration to avoid what side effect?

8. Which genetic deficiency causes osteopetrosis?

9. "Erlenmeyer flask" bones on x-ray suggest what disease?

10. What is the likely cause of cranial nerve palsies in a patient with osteopetrosis?

11. When considering osteomalacia and osteoporosis, which has defective bone mineralization, and which has reduced bone mass?

12. What condition has normal osteoid matrix accumulation around trabeculae with absent mineralization?

13. How does vitamin D deficiency in an adult affect bone mineralization?

14. What is craniotabes? Rachitic rosary?

15. The abnormal bone architecture seen in Paget's disease is caused by _____

_____.

16. What is the suspected cause of Paget's disease?

17. Serum studies on Paget's disease would be likely to show:

18. Name 3 significant complications of Paget's disease.

19. What are the features of the triad of McCune-Albright syndrome?

20. Compare bone mass, bone mineralization, and laboratory studies for osteoporosis and osteopetrosis.

21. Which disorder—osteomalacia or osteoporosis—would show hypocalcemia, hypophosphatemia, elevated parathyroid hormone, and alkaline phosphatase?

22. What lesion is characterized by brown tumors of the bone?

23. The combination of numerous colonic polyps and jaw osteoma suggests what syndrome?

Musculoskeletal and Connective Tissue

24. The histology of osteoid osteoma is ⎯⎯⎯⎯⎯⎯⎯⎯⎯⎯⎯⎯⎯⎯⎯⎯⎯⎯.

25. The histology of osteoblastoma most closely resembles the histology of what other tumor?

26. A radiographic study showing a "soap bubble" appearance of the distal femur suggests which tumor?

27. Describe the histology of giant cell tumor of bone.

28. An osteochondroma that goes on to develop a malignancy would most likely develop which malignancy?

29. Enchondromas are characteristically located in what part of the bone?

30. What are some of the risk factors for osteosarcoma?

31. What is the characteristic translocation of Ewing's sarcoma?

32. When comparing the locations in bone where chondrosarcoma and Ewing sarcoma arise, what is one site that is different?

33. Does lamellar or woven bone form an osteon?

34. Would you expect to find osteons in spongy or compact bone?

35. What is the difference between a Haversian canal and a canaliculi?

36. Name two synonyms for spongy bone.

37. What type of bone formation utilizes a cartilaginous precursor?

## TOPIC 5: ARTHRITIS

1. The polished, ivory-like appearance of bone in osteoarthritis is called _____.

2. Distinguish between Heberden's nodes and Bouchard's nodes in osteoarthritis.

3. What would biopsy of a pannus from a joint involved with rheumatoid arthritis show?

4. Contrast the timing of stiffness and pain in osteoarthritis and rheumatoid arthritis.

5. What term describes the cluster of rheumatoid arthritis, splenomegaly, and neutropenia?

6. What lung diseases can be part of the disease process of Felty's syndrome?

7. Which laboratory studies are helpful in the diagnosis of rheumatoid arthritis?

8. What characteristic deformity of the metacarpophalangeal joints occurs in rheumatoid arthritis?

9. What characteristic lesions of the proximal interphalangeal joint are seen in rheumatoid arthritis?

10. What crystals are deposited in joints and other tissues in gout?

11. What joint is classically affected in gout?

12. Describe the appearance of gout crystals.

13. Lesch-Nyhan syndrome patients develop gout because _____

   _____.

14. Match the gout drugs and targets listed below.

| Drug | Target |
|------|--------|
| Colchicine | |
| | Xanthine oxidase |
| Probenecid | |
| | COX-2 |

15. In pseudogout, what shape are the crystals, and what are their properties?

16. Name 3 important causes of infectious arthritis.

17. Name 2 causes of chronic infectious arthritis.

18. Seronegative arthropathies are often associated with which HLA type?

19. What condition often affects the fingers in psoriatic arthritis?

20. What bones and joints are commonly affected in ankylosing spondylitis? What are their limitations? What characteristic appearance is seen on x-ray?

21. Reactive arthritis is considered to be an autoimmune reaction most commonly precipitated by exposure to _____ pathogens.

22. What is the classic triad of reactive arthritis (Reiter syndrome)?

23. Identify the drugs in the following diagram.

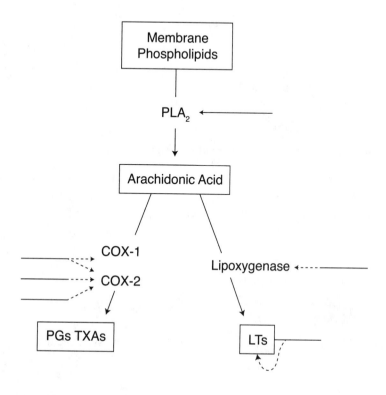

24. Name the only NSAID that irreversibly inhibits cyclooxygenase.

25. Identify the drug with analgesic and antipyretic properties that lacks anti-inflammatory effects.

26. Patients taking 6-mercaptopurine would require what dosage adjustment if allopurinol were added to the regimen?

## TOPIC 6: AUTOIMMUNE AND CONNECTIVE TISSUE DISEASES

1.  What clinical triad is typical of Sjögren's syndrome?

2.  What autoantibodies are associated with Sjögren's syndrome?

3.  What population does Sjögren's syndrome tend to affect?

4.  How does sicca syndrome differ from Sjögren's syndrome?

5.  Immune complex deposition onto heart valves in SLE can cause what condition?

6.  The presence of which autoantibodies suggests the diagnosis of systemic lupus erythematosus?

7.  Antiphospholipid antibodies target protein C and thrombin, producing a hypercoagulable state. Is the PTT prolonged, normal, or decreased?

8.  Name 3 hematologic disorders that lupus patients can develop.

9.  Immune complex depositions in the kidney in lupus can cause what pattern on histology?

10. The antiphospholipid antibodies of lupus can cause false-positive results in which tests?

11. Exposure to hydralazine and procainamide may induce formation of what antibody in patients with drug-induced SLE?

12. What is the underlying pathology of sarcoidosis?

13. What chest pathology is seen in sarcoidosis?

14. What enzyme may be elevated in the blood of patients with sarcoidosis?

15. A decrease in sensitivity of which test for tuberculosis is seen in sarcoidosis?

16. What are characteristic histologic features of sarcoidosis?

17. Describe the muscular weakness usually seen in polymyalgia rheumatica. What is found on laboratory studies?

Musculoskeletal and Connective Tissue

18. Elevation of which lab test is generally characteristic of the myositis disorders?

19. What histology is seen in polymyositis?

20. What histology is seen in dermatomyositis?

21. What can be seen on physical examination of patients with dermatomyositis?

22. There is an increased risk for _____ in dermatomyositis.

23. What autoantibody is specific for dermatomyositis?

24. In myasthenia gravis, what happens to muscle weakness with prolonged use?

25. What tumor is associated with myasthenia gravis?

26. What is the target of the autoantibodies of Lambert-Eaton syndrome?

27. What happens with repetitive nerve stimulation testing in Lambert-Eaton syndrome?

28. What autoantibody is associated with diffuse scleroderma?

29. In CREST syndrome, CREST stands for:

30. What autoantibodies are associated with CREST syndrome?

31. Identify the drugs that target tumor necrosis factor-alpha (TNF-$\alpha$).

    Recombinant TNF receptor = _____

    TNF antibody drugs = _____

# RESPIRATORY MEDICINE

## TOPIC 1: RESPIRATORY ANATOMY

1. Name the vertebral body levels where the esophagus, aorta, and inferior vena cava pass through the diaphragm.

2. Name 2 additional structures that also pass through the aortic hiatus.

3. Name 2 additional structures that also pass through the esophageal hiatus.

4. What are the 3 ventral rami that contribute to the phrenic nerves?

5. Name 2 muscles used in quiet breathing.

6. Apart from the diaphragm, name 3 muscles used in labored inspiration.

7. Name 2 muscles used in labored expiration.

8. What muscle is fatigued in a patient with paradoxical breathing?

9. What is the key physical sign observed during paradoxical breathing, and what does it indicate?

10. State the 2 major divisions of the respiratory system and the primary differences between them.

11. What structures mark the beginning and the end of the anatomic dead space?

12. Name the 3 components of the respiratory zone in the lung.

13. Name 2 structures which may compress the trachea.

14. Name 2 causes of carina displacement.

15. What is the arrangement of cartilage in the:

a)  Trachea?


b)  Bronchi?


c)  Bronchioles?


16. What key structural component in the trachea and main stem bronchi does not exist in bronchioles, and what is the functional implication of this?


17. Which component of the respiratory tree contributes most to pulmonary resistance?


18. Complete the following table.

| Features | Right Lung | Left Lung |
|---|---|---|
| Number of lobes? | | |
| Horizontal lobe present? | | |
| Lingula present? | | |
| Relationship of pulmonary artery to main stem bronchus? | | |

19. For each of the following positions, where will an aspirated foreign object tend to lodge?

| Body Position | Location of Aspirated Object |
|---|---|
| Upright | |
| Supine | |
| Lying on the right | |
| Lying on the left | |

20. Name 2 anatomic reasons why an aspirated foreign object tends to pass into the right main bronchus rather than the left.

21. How many bronchopulmonary segments are in the right and left lungs?

22. Name 3 vascular components found in each segment.

23. Name 2 main cell types found in the respiratory epithelium.

24. Name 4 functions of a Clara cell.

25. Complete the following table.

| Features | Type 1 Pneumocyte | Type 2 Pneumocyte |
|---|---|---|
| Forms 97% of alveolar surface | | |
| Secretes surfactant | | |
| A stem cell for alveolar epithelium | | |
| Part of blood-gas barrier | | |
| Contains lamellar bodies in apical cytoplasm | | |

## TOPIC 2: RESPIRATORY MECHANICS AND PULMONARY CIRCULATION

1.  A _____ : _____ ratio that is >2 indicates adequate lung maturity in a fetus. _____ are given to the mother to stimulate lung maturity in the fetus.

2.  _____ is a compound released from mast cells that causes bronchoconstriction. Another class of compounds that cause bronchoconstriction and are generated during the course of asthma and allergic reactions are the _____.

3.  Name and define the 4 lung volumes and lung capacities.

4.  _____ is a volume in the respiratory system that does not participate in gas exchange. _____ is a volume in the conducting zone. _____ are alveoli that are ventilated but not perfused, and _____ is the sum of the two. In a normal individual, there is no _____.

5.  What is alveolar ventilation if a subject has a 600 ml tidal volume, 200 ml anatomic dead space, and a respiratory rate of 10 breaths/min?

6.  Breathing room air, at the end of a normal tidal inspiration, the $PO_2$ and $PCO_2$ in the conducting zone (anatomic dead space) are approximately _____ mm Hg and _____ mm Hg, respectively.

7. At rest, the lungs have an _____ recoil, while the chest has an _____ recoil. When these forces are balanced, i.e., the same, the respiratory system is at _____.

8. At low lung volumes, _____ of the lungs is high, while _____ is low. At high lung volumes, _____ is low, while _____ is high.

9. Name a disease that increases lung compliance, and name a disease that reduces lung compliance.

10. Low alveolar $PO_2$ causes _____ of the arterioles perfusing hypoxic alveoli, thereby diverting blood flow away from the hypoxic region.

11. The rate of gas diffusion across the alveoli is directly related to the _____ _____ and _____, and inversely related to the _____ of the barrier.

12. Define perfusion-limited gas exchange, and name the prototypical gas that exhibits this characteristic.

13. Define diffusion-limited gas exchange and give the prototypical gas that exhibits this characteristic.

14. Pulmonary vascular resistance is lowest at _____.

15. State the 2 factors that determine $O_2$ delivery to tissues.

# TOPIC 3: NORMAL OXYGENATION

1.  Write the equation used to estimate alveolar $PO_2$ ($PAO_2$).

2.  Name the 4 endogenously produced factors that reduce hemoglobin's affinity for $O_2$.

3.  A patient has a normal arterial $PO_2$ and hemoglobin concentration, yet $O_2$ content is well below normal. What are the 2 most likely causes of this?

4.  Describe the "chloride shift" that occurs in the red blood cell at both the tissues and the lungs.

## TOPIC 4: HYPOXEMIA

1. What is the first step in determining the cause of hypoxemia? If the outcome is normal, what is the cause?

2. What is the common characteristic for the hypoxemia caused by $\dot{V}_A/Q$ mismatch, diffusion impairment, and right-to-left shunts? What differentiates shunts from the other 2?

3. Fill in the following table with arrows to compare and contrast the apex (top) and base (bottom) of the lung in an upright individual.

| | $\dot{V}_A$ | Q | $\dot{V}_A/Q$ | $PAO_2$ | $PACO_2$ |
|---|---|---|---|---|---|
| Apex | | | | | |
| Base | | | | | |

4. Describe the immediate responses that occur when one ascends to high altitude.

5.  Predict the physiologic compensations and problems that arise if a subject stays at high altitude for an extended period of time.

6.  Discuss the primary respiratory changes that occur with exercise.

# TOPIC 5: OBSTRUCTIVE LUNG DISEASE

1.  Is a decrease in all lung volumes more characteristic of obstructive lung disease or restrictive lung disease?

2.  A decrease in _____ is the most diagnostic marker indicating obstructive disease.

3.  Fill in the following table to compare and contrast obstructive vs. restrictive lung disease.

| | FEV$_1$/FVC | FVC | TLC | FRC | RV |
|---|---|---|---|---|---|
| Obstructive | | | | | |
| Restrictive | | | | | |

4.  Measurement of mucous gland thickness divided by thickness of bronchial wall gives what index?

5.  What enzyme is most responsible for the destruction of the interstitium of the lungs in emphysema?

6.  Which form of emphysema is associated with alpha-1-antitrypsin deficiency? Chronic smoking?

7.  Name 2 conditions that predispose for bronchiectasis.

8.  What test can be helpful in the diagnosis of asthma?

## TOPIC 6: RESTRICTIVE LUNG DISEASE

1.  What is the main difference on pulmonary function testing between obstructive lung disease and restrictive lung disease?

2.  Name 4 or more examples of diseases that produce restrictive lung diseases.

3.  What happens to angiotensin-converting enzyme in sarcoidosis?

4.  What histology is associated with sarcoidosis?

5.  The decreased diffusion capacity in the lungs seen in idiopathic pulmonary fibrosis is due to what process?

6.  Name 2 diseases that can cause both glomerulonephritis and pulmonary hemorrhage.

7.  What is the origin of the malignant cell in eosinophilic granuloma?

Respiratory Medicine

8. Name 3 drugs that are frequently implicated as causes of pulmonary fibrosis.

9. Hypersensitivity pneumonitis typically produces what pulmonary features?

10. Eggshell calcification of hilar lymph nodes is typical of what lung disease?

11. A golden-brown body resembling a dumbbell in a microscopic sample from a lung biopsy would most likely be due to what disorder? What cancers are more likely in these patients?

12. What process causes the pulmonary edema in adult respiratory distress syndrome?

13. Which experiences a greater pressure from the walls, a small alveolus or a large alveolus?

14. What is the principal component of surfactant?

15. What value of the lecithin:sphingomyelin level indicates lung maturity?

16. What are some risk factors for neonatal respiratory distress syndrome?

17. What are some risk factors for adult respiratory distress syndrome?

18. Damage to what type of cells in the lung is most important in causing adult respiratory distress syndrome?

19. What finding would typically be seen on chest x-ray in adult respiratory distress syndrome?

## TOPIC 7: PNEUMONIA AND ASSOCIATED PATHOGENS

1.  What is the most common cause of lobar pneumonia?

2.  Bronchopneumonia tends to involve which lung structure(s)?

3.  What are common causes of bronchopneumonia?

4.  What are the common causes of interstitial pneumonia?

5.  What important diseases are caused by *Streptococcus pneumoniae*?

6.  Patients with functional or true asplenia are at high risk for developing pneumonia with what organism?

7.  What type of *Haemophilus influenzae* has a successful vaccine?

8.  What is the capsule of *H. influenzae* type B composed of?

9. List the growth requirements for *(H) influenzae*. What culture media are these grown in?

10. How is *Legionella pneumophila* transmitted?

11. List the clinical triad of legionnaires' disease.

12. What is an unusual characteristic of *Legionella* pneumonia?

13. Name the agar that can allow for the growth of *Legionella*.

14. Name the class of drugs commonly used to treat *Legionella*.

15. List at least 2 risk factors for infections with *Pseudomonas aeruginosa*.

16. List the mechanism of action of the *Pseudomonas* exotoxin.

17. What organism can notably cause both ventilator-associated pneumonia and swimmer's ear (external otitis)?

18. What are the skin lesions that can occur in *Pseudomonas* sepsis?

Respiratory Medicine

19. Place an X by each characteristic or lab test that applies to *Pseudomonas aeruginosa*.

| | |
|---|---|
| Oxidase negative | |
| Lactose fermenter | |
| Endotoxin | |
| Exotoxin | |
| Blue-green pigment | |
| Catalase | |

20. Name 2 biochemical differences between Chlamydia and most bacteria.

21. Name the infectious form of Chlamydia.

22. Name the replicative form of Chlamydia.

23. What diseases are caused by *Chlamydia trachomatis*?

24. What are 2 distinctive features about the structure of *Mycoplasma*?

Respiratory Medicine

25. Why can't *Mycoplasma* be treated with penicillins or cephalosporins?

26. What serologic test can be used to confirm *Mycoplasma* infection?

## TOPIC 8: FUNGAL RESPIRATORY INFECTIONS

1. Dimorphic fungi are a mold at (list temperature) _____

   Dimorphic fungi are a yeast at (list temperature) _____

2. Name the primary treatment for the systemic fungal infections.

3. For each characteristic listed, write if it applies to *Histoplasma* (H), *Blastomyces* (B), *Paracoccidioi-des* (P), or *Coccidioides* (C).

| Characteristic | Systemic mycoses |
|---|---|
| Latin America | |
| Fungus flu | |
| Broad-based budding yeast | |
| Southwestern United States | |
| Intracellular yeast in macrophages | |
| Desert bumps | |
| Ship's steering wheel | |
| Spherule | |
| Ohio-Mississippi River Valley | |
| Bird or bat feces | |
| East of the Mississippi | |
| Dissemination to the skin | |

4. Name the causative agent of tinea versicolor: _____. A KOH mount from a patient with tinea versicolor would reveal what types of structures? Draw or describe the structures.


5. For each tinea listed, write the location where each is found.

   • Tinea corporis    _____

   • Tinea cruris       _____

   • Tinea unguinum    _____

   • Tinea barbae       _____

   • Tinea pedis        _____


6. List the 3 genera associated with cutaneous fungal infections.


7. List the *Candida* morphologies observed at the following temperatures.

   • 20°C _____

   • 37°C _____


8. List at least 2 diseases associated with recurrent *Candida* infections.


9. List 3 disease states associated with *Aspergillus* infection.


10. Draw or describe the *Aspergillus* fungi.

11. List the natural environment(s) for *Cryptococcus neoformans*.

12. List the *Cryptococcus neoformans* morphologies observed at the following temperatures.

    20°    _____

    37°    _____

13. List the patients at risk for *Mucor* infections.

14. Draw or describe the *Mucor* fungus.

15. *Pneumocystis jiroveci* is associated with diffuse pneumonia in what patient population?

16. Prophylaxis for *Pneumocystis* should begin at what CD4+ T cell count?

17. Name the causative agent of Rose Gardener's disease.

18. Describe the diagnostic yeast form of *Sporothrix*.

# TOPIC 9: VIRAL RESPIRATORY INFECTIONS

1. Name 2 viral symmetries.

2. Which type of viral capsid is always enveloped?

3. Viral envelopes are derived from which cellular structure?

4. Reassortment of viral genomes can occur only with which types of viruses, in general?

5. What is the most important clinical example of viral reassortment?

6. Define complementation.

7. Define phenotypic mixing.

8. List the vaccine types in order of immunogenicity.

9. List the vaccine type(s) that are safe to give to immunocompromised patients.

10. Name the only DNA virus family that is single-stranded.

Respiratory Medicine

11. List the DNA viruses that have a circular genome.

12. Name the only RNA virus family that is double-stranded.

13. For each virus family listed, write "+" if the virus family is positive-stranded RNA or "–" if the virus family is negative-stranded RNA. Place an "S" in the box for each family that is segmented.

| Virus Family | RNA Genome + or – |
|---|---|
| Reoviridae | |
| Coronaviridae | |
| Orthomyxoviridae | |
| Paramyxoviridae | |
| Retroviridae | |
| Caliciviridae | |
| Bunyaviridae | |
| Arenaviridae | |
| Herpesviridae | |
| Rhabdoviridae | |
| Filoviridae | |
| Flaviviridae | |
| Togaviridae | |
| Picornaviridae | |

14. Name the only DNA virus that replicates in the cytoplasm.

15. Name the RNA virus(s) that replicate in the nucleus.

16. Name the most common causative agent of the common cold.

17. List the 2 influenza viral proteins found in the viral envelope.

18. List the functions of the above 2 molecules.

19. Name the pathology common to all paramyxoviruses. What specific viral protein is associated with this pathology?

# TOPIC 10: LUNG CANCER AND PLEURAL EFFUSIONS

1.  Which organisms are likely to cause lung abscesses?

2.  What are some of the causes of cavitary lesions of the lung?

3.  Compare the protein content of transudative effusions with that of exudative effusions.

4.  What causes transudative effusions?

5.  Bilateral obliteration of the costophrenic angles can be seen in what condition?

6.  Cirrhosis patients tend to accumulate extravascular fluid in what sites?

7.  In what conditions can collagen vascular disease produce exudative effusions?

8.  How do the laboratory studies on transudates and exudates differ?

9. What is the most common cancer found in the lung?

10. Popcorn calcification in a coin lesion on chest x-ray would be more likely to be malignant or non-malignant?

11. What are some complications of lung cancer?

12. What would be likely to cause hypercalcemia in a patient with lung cancer?

13. Keratin pearls and intracellular bridges in a biopsy from a lung nodule suggest what tumor histology?

14. Hypertrophic osteoarthropathy would most likely be seen in which type of lung cancer?

15. Biopsy of a lung mass demonstrates sheets of small blue cells, which suggests what tumor?

16. What paraneoplastic syndromes are associated with small cell carcinoma?

17. From which cells does small cell carcinoma arise?

18. A primary lung cancer with many pleomorphic giant cells on microscopy would most likely be what cancer?

19. What cardiac problems can carcinoid tumors cause?

20. What tumor might cause extensive involvement of the pleura and show many areas of calcification?

21. What does the presence of ptosis, miosis, anhidrosis, and hoarseness in a patient with cancer involving the lung suggest?

22. A patient with a lung cancer who develops hyponatremia would most likely have what form of lung cancer?

# TOPIC 11: PULMONARY HYPERTENSION AND PULMONARY EMBOLISM

1.  What pressures in the pulmonary artery define pulmonary hypertension?

2.  What is the histopathology of vessels in pulmonary hypertension?

3.  What mutation is associated with primary pulmonary hypertension?

4.  What are the cardiac complications of pulmonary hypertension?

5.  Name 3 or more causes of secondary pulmonary hypertension.

6.  Central sleep apnea occurs because of cessation of signals from what brain site?

7.  How can obstructive sleep apnea cause pulmonary hypertension?

8.  When compared to normal sleep patterns, the sleep patterns in obstructive sleep apnea show which characteristics?

9. Which medications are useful for treatment of pulmonary hypertension?

10. What is the most important cause of fat emboli?

11. What are typical presenting complaints for pulmonary embolism?

12. In the context of deep venous thrombosis, what term is used for the combination of stasis, hyper-coagulability, and endothilial injury?

13. What is a physical sign of deep venous thrombosis in the leg?

# CARDIOLOGY

## TOPIC 1: CARDIAC OUTPUT

1.  In general, if an arteriole vasoconstricts, blood flow _____, pressure upstream from the site of the constriction _____, while pressure downstream from the site of the constriction _____.

2.  In general, if an arteriole vasodilates, blood flow _____, pressure upstream from the site of the constriction _____, while pressure downstream from the site of the constriction _____.

3.  When considering whole body hemodynamics, MAP equals _____ times _____.

4.  The velocity of blood is highest in the _____ and lowest in _____.

5. Fill in the table below for adrenergic receptors.

| Receptor | G Protein | Signal Transduction | Vascular Effect | Heart Effect |
|---|---|---|---|---|
| $\alpha_1$ | | | | |
| $\alpha_2$ | | | | |
| $\beta_1$ | | | | |
| $\beta_2$ | | | | |

6. Cardiac output equals _____ times _____.

7. The following data were obtained from subject A:

   $O_2$ consumption = 300 ml$O_2$/min

   Hb concentration = 15 mg/dl

   Arterial $O_2$ saturation = 99%

   Mixed-venous $O_2$ saturation = 75%

   What is the cardiac output of subject A?

8. Independent of heart rate (HR), list the 3 factors that influence ventricular output.

9. Discuss the mechanisms by which β-1 receptor stimulation increases contractility of the heart. How is this process altered by the inotropic agents inamrinone and milrinone?

10. Discuss the mechanisms by which digoxin increases contractility of the heart.

11. What is preload for the ventricle and how does it impact ventricular output?

12. Stroke volume divided by end-diastolic volume gives _____, which is a clinical marker of myocardial contractility.

13. List the 2 factors that directly determine mean systemic filling pressure. Also describe their relationship with venous return.

14. Indicate what happens to venous return when arterioles vasoconstrict or vasodilate.

## TOPIC 2: THE CARDIAC CYCLE

1. On a basic level, what are the 2 things the heart does during systole?

2. On a basic level, what are the 2 things the heart does during diastole?

3. Indicate the event/phase/representation of the labeled parts of the left ventricular pressure-volume loop provided below.

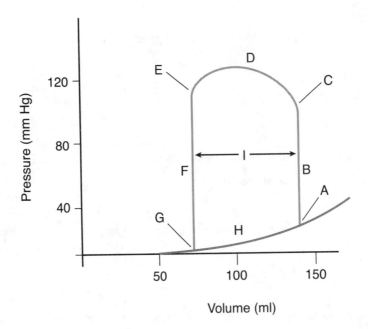

4. Fill in the blanks using the pressure-volume loop depicted above. A change in volume at point

   _____ indicates a Frank-Starling alteration in function. A change in pressure at point

   _____ would indicate a change in _____. The first heart sound (S1) occurs at

   point _____, while the second heart sound (S2) occurs at point _____.

5.  Ventricular function can be shifted by 4 basic factors. Note them on the graph below.

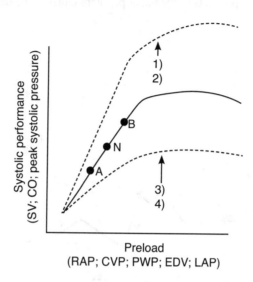

6.  Using the ventricular function curve above, indicate the shift (1/2, 3/4, N → B, or N → A, with N representing normal) that directly occurs (no compensation) in response to:

1) Hemorrhage _____

2) Propranolol _____

3) Dobutamine _____

4) Standing upright _____

5) Myocardial ischemia _____

6) Phenylephrine _____

7) Entering space (zero gravity) _____

8) Lying down _____

9) Prazosin _____

10) Cholera toxin _____.

7. Below is a depiction of a right atrial/venous pulse pressure trace. Indicate what occurs during each labeled portion, and note on the picture the valve problem causing the depicted alteration.

(A)

(C)

(X)

(V)

(Y)

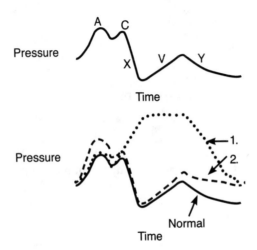

8. Fill in the table below for the arterial baroreflex.

| Arterial Blood Pressure | Baroreceptor Activity | Parasympathetic Activity | Sympathetic Activity | HR | TPR |
|---|---|---|---|---|---|
| Increase | | | | | |
| Decrease | | | | | |

9. Discuss the long-term regulation of blood pressure.

# TOPIC 3: REGULATION OF BLOOD FLOW AND FLUID EXCHANGE

1. _____is the maintenance of a relatively constant flow despite changes in pressure. _____ and _____ mechanisms cause this effect.

2. Although the brain is a good autoregulator, an increase in _____ will vasodilate the cerebral circulation.

3. Considering the Fick principle related to $O_2$ consumption, what unique characteristic does the heart at rest have compared to the other organs?

4. Describe how the pulmonary circulation responds to low $O_2$ differently than systemic vessels.

5. Given the following variables, what is the net force for filtration and what direction is water moving?

    Pc = 32 mm Hg      $\pi$c = 30
    Pif = –3          $\pi$if = 2

6. Hydrostatic pressure in the capillary is directly related to what 3 variables?

7. Compare and contrast transudative and exudative fluid flux.

8. Identify the agonist from the receptor(s) it stimulates.

| Drug | Receptor(s) |
|------|-------------|
|      | $\alpha_1, \alpha_2, \beta_1$ |
|      | $\alpha_1$ |
|      | $\beta_1, \beta_2$ |
|      | $\alpha_1, \alpha_2, \beta_1, \beta_2$ |
|      | $D_1, \beta_1, \alpha_1$ |
|      | $\beta_1$ |

9. Use the Vaughan-Williams classification system to classify the drugs below.

| Drug | Classification |
|------|----------------|
| Lidocaine |  |
| Amiodarone |  |
| Procainamide |  |
| Esmolol |  |
| Verapamil |  |
| Sotalol |  |
| Quinidine |  |

# TOPIC 4: CARDIAC ELECTROPHYSIOLOGY

1. Name/indicate what is occurring at the 4 labeled points in the cardiac myocyte (A–D).

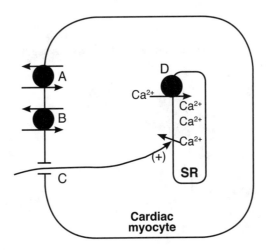

2. Name the ion that is primarily responsible for the voltage or voltage change at the 5 labeled points (0–4) on the cardiac action potential.

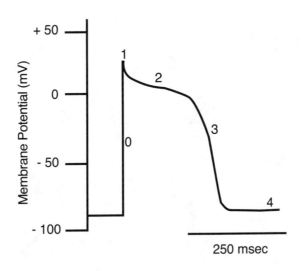

Cardiology

3.  Discuss the ionic currents responsible for phase 4 (pacemaker potential) and phase 0 in the SA and AV node.

4.  On the ECG trace below, label the various waves, intervals, and segments, as well as a brief explanation about how they are caused.

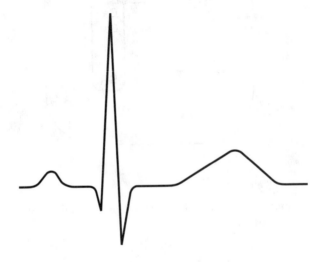

# TOPIC 5: ARRHYTHMIAS

1. A long _____ can lead to torsades de pointes.

2. What is a delta wave, and what arrhythmia does it indicate?

3. Define first-, second-, and third-degree heart blocks.

4. Prior to starting therapy with amiodarone, 3 organ function tests should be performed. List each test and the side effect for which you would monitor.

| Test | Side Effect |
|------|-------------|
|      |             |
|      |             |
|      |             |

## TOPIC 6: HEART SOUNDS

1.  Fill in the chart below to indicate common causes for altered splitting of the second heart sound.

| | Wide | Fixed | Paradoxical |
|---|---|---|---|
| Condition | 1)<br><br>2) | 1) | 1)<br><br>2) |

2.  For valve stenosis, it is important to remember that _____ and _____ upstream of the defective valve increase.

3.  List the 4 valve pathologies that can create a systolic murmur.

4.  List the 4 valve pathologies that can create a diastolic murmur.

5.  An ejection "click" occurs in what valve pathology?

6.  An opening "snap" occurs in what valve pathology?

# TOPIC 7: HYPERTENSION

1. Name some long-term consequences of hypertension.


2. What is the most common cause of renal artery stenosis in an older patient? In a young female patient?


3. Decreased pressure in the renal afferent arteriole triggers secretion of what enzyme by the juxtaglomerular cells? What does this enzyme do?


4. Compared with a normal person, how do the number of peripheral arterioles change in a patient with primary hypertension? The arteriolar wall thickness? The total peripheral resistance?


5. Hypertrophy of the wall of which cardiac chamber is most prominent in longstanding cases of hypertension?


6. What are some other consequences of long-standing hypertension?


7. What vessel changes characterize essential hypertension? Malignant hypertension?

8.  In hypertension, what does the term "onion-skinning" refer to?

9.  What types of material does the necrotic core contain in an advanced atherosclerotic plaque?

10. What are locations of 4 clinically important aneurysms?

11. What type of degeneration in the aorta is occurring in cystic medial necrosis?

12. What finding on chest x-ray is most characteristic of aortic dissection?

13. A hypertensive patient with diabetes would benefit more from what type of drug?

14. Complete the table below on cardiovascular drugs.

| Drug/Drug Class | Property |
|---|---|
| | Diuretic, ↑LDLs |
| | Antiarrhythmic CCBs |
| | $\alpha_2$ agonist, (+) Coombs test |
| | Irreversible $\alpha$-blocker |
| | Diuretic, ↓ cardiac remodeling |
| | Most cardiodepressant CCB |
| | Useful in BPH and hypertension |

# TOPIC 8: LIPID METABOLISM

1. What is the function of bile?

2. Name the enterocyte enzyme responsible for breaking down the following dietary lipids at the brush border:

    (A) Triglycerides

    (B) Cholesterol esters

    (C) Phospholipids

3. Which lipase enzyme catalyzes the breakdown of dietary triglycerides in the small intestine?

4. Which lipase enzyme catalyzes the breakdown of triglycerides circulating in chylomicrons and VLDL?

5. Which lipase enzyme catalyzes the breakdown of triglycerides stored in adipocytes?

6. Which apoprotein mediates chylomicron secretion from intestinal enterocytes into lymphatic vessels?

7. What lipids and what lipoproteins are elevated in the blood in familial lipoprotein lipase deficiency? Familial hypercholesterolemia? Hepatic overproduction of VLDL?

8. Which apoproteins are lacking in abetalipoproteinemia?

9. Identify the lipid-lowering drug corresponding to the mechanism of action:

    (A) Activates PPAR-α      _____

    (B) Causes flushing and itching      _____

    (C) Absorption of vitamins A, D, E, K      _____

    (D) Cholesterol absorption in GI tract      _____

    (E) Monitor LFTs and creatine kinase      _____

# TOPIC 9: ATHEROSCLEROSIS

1. Atherosclerosis is a disease of which vessels?

2. What 2 substances contribute to smooth muscle migration out of the media toward the intima in atherosclerosis?

3. Where are berry aneurysms most commonly located?

4. What is the difference between Stanford A and Stanford B dissections?

5. What can happen if a dissecting aneurysm spreads back toward the heart to involve the coronary arteries?

6. What are 3 risk factors for aortic dissection?

7. What is Prinzmetal's angina?

8. What are 4 clinical syndromes associated with ischemic heart disease?

# TOPIC 10: ISCHEMIC HEART DISEASE

1. What is the first histologic sign of myocardial infarction (MI)?

2. When does neutrophilic infiltration of myocardium peak in an MI?

3. When does maximal softening of the necrotic myocardium occur after an MI?

4. Of troponin I, CK-MB, AST, and LDH, which has the most cardiac specificity?

5. ECG showing ST elevations early on and Q waves later suggests what condition?

6. ST segment changes and Q waves in the V4-V6 leads suggest which location for an MI?

7. Pump failure with resulting hypoperfusion of all organs causes what condition?

8. Papillary muscle rupture would most likely occur how long after an MI?

9. A ventricular aneurysm can occur several weeks to months after an MI. What complications can ventricular aneurysm predispose to?

10. What condition causes a fibrinous pericarditis due to an autoimmune process?

11. List the classes of drugs used in stable angina.

12. List the classes of drugs used in vasospastic angina.

13. What is the primary therapeutic strategy for prevention of stable angina?

# TOPIC 11: CONGESTIVE HEART FAILURE AND CARDIOMYOPATHIES

1. The cardiac remodeling that occurs during the development of dilated cardiomyopathy occurs by what process?

2. Name frequently abused substances that can cause a dilated cardiomyopathy.

3. Name 2 infectious causes of dilated cardiomyopathy.

4. Roughly what percentage of hypertrophic cardiomyopathy is thought to be genetically related?

5. What mechanism causes the S4 heart sound in hypertrophic cardiomyopathy?

6. Hemochromatosis and amyloidosis tend to cause what type of cardiomyopathy?

7. Decreased renal blood flow in the setting of congestive heart failure can cause edema by what mechanism?

8. Central venous congestion of the liver produces what findings on intraoperative examination of the liver?

9.  What name is used for decreased pulse strength during inspiration during tamponade?


10. Identify the cellular target of each inotrope.


| Drug | Target |
|------|--------|
| Digoxin | |
| Dobutamine | |
| Inamrinone | |

# TOPIC 12: CONGENITAL HEART DISEASE

1.  What specific germ layer forms the heart?

2.  Match each heart tube dilatation, from caudal to cranial, with its postnatal fate.

| Heart Tube Dilatation | Fate |
|---|---|
| Sinus venosus right horn | Smooth right atrium |
| Sinus venosus left horn | Coronary sinus |
| Primitive atrium | Trabeculated R and L atrium |
| Primitive ventricle | Trabeculated R and L ventricle |
| Conus arteriosus | Smooth parts of L and R ventricle (outflow) |
| Truncus arteriosus | Ascending aorta and pulmonary trunk |

3.  What do cardinal veins form when they fuse?

4.  What septum divides the truncus arteriosus?

5.  If this septum does not develop in the form of a spiral, what condition develops?

6.  Name the 2 parts of the interventricular septum.

7.  What structures fuse and close the atrioventricular canals?

8. Name 2 endocardial cushion defects.

9. Which endocardial cushion defect is associated with maternal lithium use?

10. Which endocardial cushion defect results in a hypoplastic right side of the heart?

11. Which endocardial cushion defect results in an "atrialized" right ventricle?

12. Name 3 congenital heart defects that might undergo an L-to-R shunt reversal and develop the Eisenmenger syndrome and late cyanosis.

13. What is the underlying problem in Eisenmenger's syndrome?

14. Name the 2 components of the interatrial septum.

15. Which component fuses with the endocardial cushions?

16. What foramina are found in each septum?

17. What is a patient with a patent foramen ovale at risk for?

18. What is the most common atrial septal defect?

19. Fill out the table according to when sites of fetal erythropoiesis begin producing red blood cells.

| Fetal Erythropoiesis Sites | Timeline (Weeks) |
|---|---|
| Bone marrow | |
| Liver | |
| Yolk sac | |
| Spleen | |

20. What is the difference in subunit composition of fetal versus adult hemoglobin?

21. Name 2 organs that fetal circulation is designed to divert oxygenated fetal blood away from.

22. Name the shunts that bypass each organ.

23. What changes in levels of prostaglandins and oxygen tension promote closure of the ductus arteriosus?

24. List the 5 "T" titled cyanotic right-to-left shunts and 3 non-cyanotic left-to-right shunts.

| Five Cyanotic R-L Shunts | Three Non-Cyanotic L-R Shunts |
|---|---|
| 1. | 1. |
| 2. | 2. |
| 3. | 3. |
| 4. | |
| 5. | |

25. Failure of what mechanism causes persistent truncus arteriosus?

26. What 2 additional defects must be present with tricuspid atresia in order for the newborn to be viable?

27. Which of the 3 postnatal conditions that undergo the Eisenmenger syndrome results in a differential cyanosis?

28. Which part of the tetralogy of Fallot is the most important determinant of prognosis?

29. How does squatting aid an individual with Tetralogy of Fallot?

30. What are the 3 initial defects in tetralogy of Fallot? What pathology arising from the initial defects creates the 'boot-shaped' heart?

31. In what population is transposition of the great vessels commonly seen?

32. What 3 additional defects must be present for a newborn with transposition of the great arteries to be viable?

33. Which form of a coarctation of the aorta is associated with Turner's syndrome?

34. Which coarctation type will be associated with "rib notching?"

35. Which coarctation type will show cyanosis in the lower limbs?

36. Which coarctation type will show evidence of higher blood pressures in the upper limbs and lower blood pressures in the lower limbs?

37. Which coarctation type is associated with a bicuspid aortic valve?

38. What structure in an adult corresponds to the ductus arteriosus in a fetus?

39. Match each congenital heart condition with a frequent association or cause. Condition choices may be used more than once:

(A)   Tetralogy of Fallot

(B)   ASD or VSD

(C)   PDA

(D)   Transposition of great vessels

(E)   Preductal coarctation of aorta

(F)   Truncus arteriosus

(G)   Aortic insufficiency

(H)   Endocardial cushion defect


1.   Down syndrome

2.   Marfan's syndrome

3.   Infant of diabetic mother

4.   22q11 syndrome (DiGeorge)

5.   Congenital rubella

6.   Turner's syndrome

# TOPIC 13: INFECTION-RELATED HEART DISEASE

1.  Circle the Gram-positive cell wall.

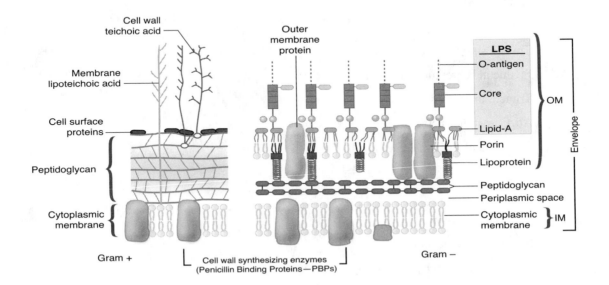

2.  Fill in the flow chart with the Gram-positive cocci.

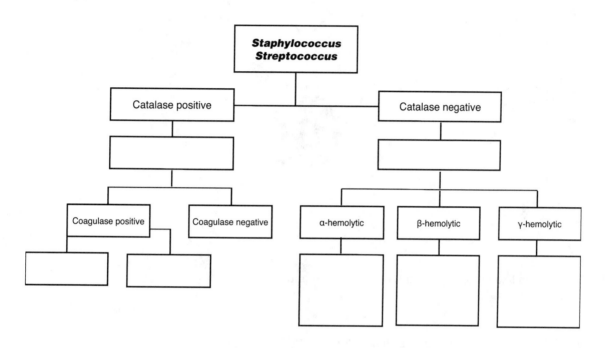

3.  List the substrate for myeloperoxidase.

4.  Discuss why patients with chronic granulomatous disease have frequent infections with catalase-positive bacteria.

5. Describe the function of protein A produced by *Staphylococcus aureus*. A drawing is shown.

6. List the toxin made by *S. aureus* that is a superantigen (sAg).

7. Discuss the mechanism by which the sAg leads to shock.

8. List the major surface type that *Staphylococcus epidermidis* binds to.

9. Discuss the mechanism by which viridans streptococci adhere to damaged heart valves.

10. Name the compound that enterococci can be selectively grown in.

11. Name the drug of choice for enterococci infection.

12. Name the drug of choice for vancomycin-resistant enterococci infection.

13. Name the co-morbidity associated with endocarditis caused by *Streptococcus bovis*.

14. List at least 3 common symptoms of endocarditis.

15. *Staphylococcus aureus* typically causes what type of endocarditis? *Streptococcus viridans*?

16. What type of endocarditis is associated with pancreatic cancer?

17. For each characteristic listed, place an "A" if the characteristic is associated with acute endocarditis or an "S" if it is associated with subacute endocarditis.

| Characteristic | Type of Endocarditis |
| --- | --- |
| Affects previously damaged heart valves | |
| Affects normal valves | |
| *S. aureus* is the most common causative agent | |
| High virulence | |
| Low virulence | |
| Streptococcus viridans are common in this group | |

18. List the HACEK organisms.

19. Where are the HACEK organisms normally found?

20. Name the valve most commonly associated with endocarditis.

21. Name the valve most commonly associated with endocarditis in an IV drug user.

22. List the autoimmune disease associated with Libman-Sacks endocarditis.

23. Libman-Sacks endocarditis can involve sterile vegetations on both sides of which heart valves?

24. Name the stage of syphilis at which heart disease is usually detected.

25. What valves are affected in rheumatic fever?

26. What is required for a diagnosis of rheumatic fever?

27. What is required for a diagnosis of rheumatic fever?

# TOPIC 14: VASCULITIS AND CARDIOVASCULAR TUMORS

1. What are some of the common causes of varicose veins?

2. The blanching and then cyanosis seen in Raynaud's disease is due to what process?

3. What 3 processes are typical of Wegener's granulomatosis?

4. C-ANCA are antibodies directed against what type of cells?

5. In C-ANCA, where does the antibody bind in the cell? How about in P-ANCA?

6. Wegener's disease is associated with which form of ANCA?

7. How does microscopic polyangiitis differ from Wegener's disease?

8. What disease is characterized by congenital capillary malformations that may involve the face and leptomeninges?

9. Henoch-Schönlein purpura is linked to which virus?

10. The crescent formation seen in the rapidly progressive glomerulonephritis of Henoch-Schönlein purpura is most closely related to which type of immune complexes?

11. What is an alternate name for Buerger's disease? Name a risk factor.

12. What is the most feared complication of Kawasaki disease?

13. Which hepatitis virus is associated with polyarteritis nodosa? What can be seen on angiography?

14. What is the most common site of involvement of Takayasu's arteritis?

15. Which cell is characteristically found in biopsies of temporal arteritis?

16. What musculoskeletal disease is often associated with temporal arteritis?

17. Temporal arteritis can by complicated by which ocular problem?

18. What might cause a large, benign, pink-to-reddish, raised lesion seen on the cheek of a 1-year-old?

19. What lymphatic lesion of the neck is associated with Turner's syndrome?

20. In what organ are angiosarcomas most commonly seen?

21. What are some risk factors for angiosarcoma?


22. Myxomas tend to occur in which cardiac chamber? What do they cause there?


23. What histology is seen in a cardiac myxoma?


24. What is the most common primary cardiac tumor in children?


25. Cardiac rhabdomyoma is associated with what disorder?

# GASTROENTEROLOGY

## TOPIC 1: GASTROENTEROLOGY EMBRYOLOGY AND ASSOCIATED DISORDERS

1.  What specific germ layer forms the epithelial lining of the gut tube?

2.  What germ layer forms the rest of the wall of the gut tube?

3.  Fill in the component for each gut region.

|  | Foregut | Midgut | Hindgut |
| --- | --- | --- | --- |
| Parts? | | | |
| Parasympathetic innervation? | | | |
| Sympathetic innervation? | | | |
| Referred pain site? | | | |
| Suspended by dorsal mesentery? | | | |
| Suspended by ventral mesentery? | | | |
| Amount of rotation and direction? | | | |
| Physiological herniation? | | | |

4.  Name 3 nerves that innervate the parietal peritoneum.

5.  Name 3 examples of a mesentery.

6.  What structures pass between the 2 layers of a mesentery?

7.  Name 4 parts of the gut tube that are secondarily retroperitoneal (lost a mesentery during development).

8. Name one part of the foregut, midgut, and hindgut that is suspended by a mesentery in postnatal life.

9. What 2 regions of the abdomen does the epiploic foramen connect?

10. What structures course in the anterior border of the epiploic foramen?

11. What 3 structures form the portal triad?

12. In 90% of cases the fistula in a tracheoesophageal fistula is located in what site?

13. What is the cause of a tracheoesophageal fistula?

14. Name 3 postnatal signs or symptoms of a tracheoesophageal fistula.

15. What may be evident during pregnancy in which a fetus has a tracheoesophageal fistula?

16. What physical exam finding is characteristic of hypertrophic pyloric stenosis?

17. In an infant with hypertrophic pyloric stenosis, describe the nature of the vomiting and the sign evident at the right costal margin.

18. What is one complication of a congenital diaphragmatic hernia?

19. What major anatomic problems can accompany congenital diaphragmatic hernia?

20. What is the cause of duodenal atresia?

21. For a child born with duodenal atresia, what condition might complicate the pregnancy, and what will be evident on the first day of life?

22. Duodenal atresia is associated with what syndrome?

23. What is thought to be the underlying cause of most small bowel atresias?

24. What 2 signs of small bowel atresias might be evident on x-ray?

25. At what fetal age does malrotation of the gut develop? What intestinal abnormality might develop in these patients?

26. Name 2 symptoms of volvulus.

27. At what site does gastroschisis usually develop? Are the viscera enclosed by amnion?

28. What is the cause of gastroschisis?

29. At what site is the defect typically located?

30. What is the cause of an omphalocele?

31. Through what opening does the midgut protrude in an omphalocele?

32. Name 2 other congenital abnormalities that are frequently associated with an omphalocele. What membrane encloses the herniated midgut in this condition?

33. What is the cause of Meckel's diverticulum?

34. Complete the following table.

| | Meckel's Diverticulum Characteristics |
|---|---|
| Percentage of population affected? | |
| Distance from ileocecal valve? | |
| Length? | |
| Presentation age? | |

35. Name 2 complications associated with Meckel's diverticulum.

36. What is the relationship between Meckel's diverticulum and intussusception?

37. A vitelline fistula causes a patent connection between which 2 structures?

38. What will drain through the vitelline fistula?

39. What is the cause of Hirschsprung's disease? Name the most commonly affected area of the bowel.

40. What techniques are used to diagnose Hirschsprung's disease? How does Hirschsprung's usually present in the neonatal period?

41. In what mesentery does the liver and the biliary apparatus develop?

42. What 2 remnants of this mesentery suspend the liver in postnatal life?

43. Incomplete canalization of the lumen of biliary ducts leads to what condition?

44. What is the nature of the stool and the urine in this condition?

45. What components of the pancreas do the ventral and dorsal pancreatic buds form when they fuse?

46. What forms the main pancreatic duct?

47. What is the name of the most common abnormality of the pancreas?

48. What embryologic event causes pancreas divisum?

49. How does annular pancreas cause polyhydramnios?

50. What germ layer gives rise to the spleen?

51. What 2 mesentery remnants suspend the spleen?

52. From what artery does the splenic artery arise?

## TOPIC 2: GASTROENTEROLOGY ANATOMY, HISTOLOGY, AND PHYSIOLOGY

1.  Name the 4 layers of the gut wall.

2.  What are the 3 components of the mucosa?

3.  Complete the following table.

| GI Intrinsic Innervation | Meissner's Plexus | Auerbach's Plexus |
|---|---|---|
| Location | | |
| Function | | |
| Input source(s) | | |
| Parasympathetic effects | | |
| Sympathetic effects | | |

4.  Complete the following table.

| Salivary Glands | Location | Composition and % of Saliva Volume |
|---|---|---|
| Parotid | | |
| Submandibular | | |
| Sublingual | | |

5.  Name the 4 main ionic components of saliva.

6. Name 2 digestive enzymes found in saliva.

7. What nerves control salivary secretions?

8. At what vertebral level does the esophagus traverse the diaphragm?

9. Name 4 narrow points along the length of the esophagus.

10. What is the arrangement of smooth and skeletal muscle in the upper 1/3, middle 1/3, and lower 1/3 of the esophagus?

11. What is characteristic of the epithelial lining of the esophagus?

12. Name the 3 endogenous compounds that stimulate gastric acid secretion.

13. Discuss the stimuli and interaction of the 3 compounds named in the previous question.

14. _____ is a hormone released from gastric and intestinal cells that inhibits gastrin release.

15. The pumping of $H^+$ into the lumen is an antiport $H^+$-ATPase. _____ is the ion that antiports with $H^+$.

16. In addition to $H^+$, _____ and _____ are secreted into the lumen of the stomach, thus making stomach secretions high in these electrolytes.

17. Discuss what is meant by "alkaline tide."

18. Indicate the 2 mechanisms by which drugs inhibit acid secretion by parietal cells.

19. _____ and _____ are required for complete fat digestion and absorption.

20. Name the 3 primary end products of carbohydrate digestion and the mechanism of absorption for each.

21. Protein digestion begins in the _____ via the enzyme _____.

22. _____ stimulates the pancreas to release inactive proteases that will ultimately be converted to active proteases in the _____.

23. Discuss the mechanism for the absorption of the end products of protein digestion.

24. The secretion of _____ causes Na⁺ and water to enter the lumen of the small intestine and is important for maintaining adequate hydration of the chyme.

25. Bicarbonate secretion begins in the _____, which is also the site of bile salt and B12 absorption.

26. Fill in the table below for the key GI hormones.

| Hormone | Source | Stimulus | Action |
|---------|--------|----------|--------|
| CCK | | | |
| Gastrin | | | |
| GIP | | | |
| Motilin | | | |
| Secretin | | | |

27. What are 2 types of diaphragmatic hernias seen in adults?

28. What type of inguinal hernia passes through Hesselbach's triangle, and what type passes outside of it?

## TOPIC 3: GASTROINTESTINAL PATHOLOGY

1. Malignant salivary gland tumors are most common in what age group? Benign salivary tumors are most common in what age group?

2. What percentage of pleomorphic adenomas transform into carcinomas?

3. Where is a Zenker's diverticulum located?

4. What are 2 risk factors for achalasia?

5. A "bird-beak" sign on a barium swallow study suggests what disease?

6. What is the most appropriate name for a thin circumferential "ledge" made of mucosa and submucosa, located at the squamo-columnar junction proximal to the lower esophageal sphincter?

7. Plummer-Vinson syndrome is related to deficiency of what nutrient?

8. What is the difference between Mallory-Weiss syndrome and Boerhaave's syndrome?

9. Mild non-bleeding esophageal varices can be treated with what medications?

10. What medications are used to treat gastroesophageal reflux disease (GERD)?

11. For what condition is Barrett's metaplasia a risk factor?

12. Squamous cell carcinoma most typically involves what part of the esophagus?

13. Ménétrier disease causes what histologic change?

14. Blockade of what substance can be used to treat Ménétrier disease?

15. Zollinger-Ellison syndrome can be associated with what hereditary condition?

16. What commonly used products are associated with acute gastritis?

17. What are predisposing factors for gastric stress ulcers?

18. What cells are thought to mediate parietal cell destruction in type A chronic gastritis?

19. Which bacteria are associated with type B gastritis?

20. What are the major risk factors for peptic ulcers?

21. Where in the duodenum are duodenal peptic ulcers typically located?

22. Where are gastric peptic ulcers typically located?

23. Which blood group has an increased rate of gastric carcinoma?

24. Signet-ring cells are characteristic of which type of gastric carcinoma?

25. What is the 5-year survival rate of gastric carcinoma?

26. What are some classic sites for metastasis of gastric cancer?

27. What are some of the risk factors for volvulus?

28. A "target sign" on CT of the abdomen suggests which small intestinal disease?

29. What are the HLA types associated with celiac disease (gluten sensitivity)?

30. Name 2 important disease associations for celiac disease.

31. What serologic tests can help diagnose celiac disease?

32. Tropical sprue responds to what drug class?

33. What is the causative organism of Whipple disease?

34. Are extraintestinal manifestations more common in ulcerative colitis or Crohn's disease?

35. A colon with rectal ulceration and pseudopolyp formation would be most likely to have ulcerative colitis or Crohn's disease?

36. Transmural inflammation, anal involvement, and skip lesions are characteristic of what type of inflammatory bowel disease?

37. Which type of inflammatory bowel disease confers a greater risk of cancer?

38. An acute exacerbation of ulcerative colitis that was unresponsive to 5-ASA derivatives might be treated by which type of drug?

39. What colon areas are at increased risk for ischemic bowel disease?

40. Of what are hemorrhoids composed?

41. What 2 conditions are risk factors for angiodysplasia?

42. Melanosis coli is associated with use of what drug?

43. Pseudomembranous colitis is associated with overgrowth of what bacterium?

44. Of what is the pseudomembrane of pseudomembranous colitis composed?

45. What typically begins the process leading to appendicitis?

46. How does the pain of appendicitis change with time?

47. What is the major risk factor for colonic diverticulosis?

48. Adenomatous polyps can be subclassified in what ways?

49. Familial adenomatous polyposis is associated with what gene?

50. In addition to colon cancer, what other tumors are associated with Gardner syndrome?

51. In addition to colon cancer, what other tumor is associated with Turcot syndrome?

52. Lynch syndrome differs from other hereditary colon cancer syndromes by the absence of what?

53. Which polyposis syndrome does not cause colon cancers but is associated with an increased risk of developing cancers of lungs, pancreas, breast, and uterus?

54. What dietary factors are risk factors for adenocarcinoma of the colon?

55. What configuration would colon cancer on the right side of the colon be most likely to have?

On the left side of the colon?

56. A colon cancer that invades the muscularis propria with no known metastases to lymph nodes or other sites would have what TNM stage?

57. Metastatic adenocarcinoma of the colon is often treated with what agent?

58. What are the most common locations for GI carcinoid tumors?

# TOPIC 4: LIVER AND PANCREAS PATHOLOGY

1. What is final common pathway of most causes of acute pancreatitis?

2. Laboratory studies in a case of acute pancreatitis might show what findings?

3. What is the most accurate test for acute pancreatitis?

4. What are the most important risk factors for chronic pancreatitis?

5. What finding is usually sought on x-ray and CT scan in the diagnosis of chronic pancreatitis?

6. Among pancreatic islet cell tumors, what clinical syndromes can be produced with insulinoma?

   Gastrinoma?

   Glucagonoma?

   Somatostatinoma?

   VIPoma?

7. What is the fourth most common cause of cancer death in the United States?

8. Besides a mass, what can a CT scan demonstrate in pancreatic cancer that might be helpful in diagnosis?

9. List the 3 classes of conditions that cause jaundice due to an increase in indirect (unconjugated) bilirubin.

10. List the 4 classes of conditions that cause jaundice due to an increase in direct (conjugated) bilirubin.

11. Jaundice due to hemolytic anemia can predispose to what type of gallstones?

12. Which of the hereditary hyperbilirubinemias produce conjugated hyperbilirubinemia?

    Unconjugated hyperbilirubinemia?

13. What is the difference between micronodular and macronodular cirrhosis?

14. What are some signs and symptoms of portal hypertension?

    Of liver failure?

15. What is hepatorenal syndrome?

16. What histologic features characterize alcoholic hepatitis?

17. What percentage of alcoholics develop cirrhosis?

18. Mutation of what gene is associated with Wilson disease?

19. What laboratory findings are used to diagnose Wilson disease?

20. What is the most common mutation of the HFE gene in hemochromatosis?

21. What methods are used to diagnose hemochromatosis?

22. What functions does alpha-1-antitrypsin have?

23. What finding is characteristically seen in the liver in alpha-1-antitrypsin deficiency?

24. Most cases of Reye's syndrome occur in which patients?

25. What clinical features are seen in Reye's syndrome?

26. In the pathophysiology of non-alcoholic steatohepatitis, how is oxidative stress produced?

27. What laboratory studies can be used to detect non-alcoholic steatohepatitis?

28. What are examples of diseases/factors that can lead to Budd-Chiari syndrome?

29. What does the histology in Budd-Chiari syndrome show?

30. Nutmeg pattern on gross examination of a liver suggests what disease process?

31. What is the most common primary tumor to affect liver?

32. Hepatic adenoma is associated with use of what medication?

33. What is seen histologically in hepatocellular adenoma?

34. Name some important risk factors for hepatocellular carcinoma.

35. What is a useful serum tumor marker for hepatocellular carcinoma?

36. Name 3 common primary cancers causing metastatic disease in the liver.

37. What are typical generalized symptoms of viral hepatitis?

38. What are some laboratory studies to diagnose hepatitis?

39. What are the apoptotic hepatocytes seen in viral hepatitis called?

40. What type of virus causes hepatitis A? How is it transmitted?

41. What serum studies are helpful in demonstrating hepatitis B as the cause of a patient's hepatitis?

42. What does the presence of the IgG form of HBcAb suggest?

43. What stage of hepatitis B infection would a patient have with the following profile?

    Positive HBsAg, HBeAg, HBV-DNA, and HBcAb IgG

    Negative HBsAb IgG

44. What medications can be used to treat chronic hepatitis C?

45. Hepatitis D virus replicates only in liver cells infected with what other virus?

46. In what patient population is hepatitis E virus particularly dangerous?

47. Which 2 hepatitis viruses cause acute but not chronic hepatitis?

# ENDOCRINOLOGY

## TOPIC 1: THE HYPOTHALAMIC-PITUITARY AXIS

1.  Name the secretory product of each of the following hypothalamic nuclei.

| Hypothalamic Nucleus | Secretory Product? |
|---|---|
| Supraoptic | |
| Paraventricular | |
| Arcuate | |
| Preoptic | |

2.  Fill in the table below.

| Hypothalamus | Anterior Pituitary Cell | Anterior Pituitary Hormone |
|---|---|---|
| GnRH (stimulates) | | |
| | Corticotrophs | |
| | | TSH |
| Dopamine (inhibits) | | |
| | | GH |
| | | GH |

3.  With the exception of _____, all of the hypothalamic hormones are secreted in a _____ fashion.

4.  Elevated levels of the hypothalamic hormone _____ can stimulate prolactin release. Name 4 non-hypothalamic agents that can stimulate prolactin release.

5.  What two specific subsets of ectoderm give rise to the anterior versus the posterior pituitary?

6.  Name two secretory products of the posterior pituitary.

7.  Name the tumor that may develop from a remnant of Rathke's pouch.

8.  A 28-year-old female is still unable to lactate 2 days following parturition. Examination of her records shows a difficult labor with severe postpartum hemorrhaging. This patient likely suffers from _____ and is unable to lactate because there is insufficient _____. What other hormones are likely low in this patient?

9.  What is the typical cause of Sheehan syndrome?

10. In diabetes insipidus, what symptoms and lab changes result from a decrease in the production of ADH or a decrease in responsiveness to ADH?

11. Central diabetes insipidus can be due to dysfunction in what areas of the hypothalamus?

12. Nephrogenic diabetes insipidus can be due to mutation of what gene?

13. What role does vasopressin administration play in the water deprivation test?

14. Desmopressin is used in what form of diabetes insipidus? How about hydrochlorothiazide?

15. Name 4 conditions that can cause SIADH.

16. When compared to diabetes insipidus, SIADH shows what changes in urine osmolarity and ECF osmolarity?

17. What complication can be caused by overaggressive correction of serum osmolarity in SIADH?

18. Fill in the table below to compare and contrast alterations in water homeostasis.

| | Diabetes Insipidus | Syndrome of Inappropriate ADH (SIADH) | Dehydration | Primary Polydipsia |
|---|---|---|---|---|
| Urine flow | | | | |
| Urine osmolality | | | | |
| Plasma osmolality | | | | |
| Extracellular volume | | | | |
| Intracellular volume | | | | |

19. Which 2 of the conditions in the previous question are often associated with hyponatremia?

20. The most common type of microadenoma of the pituitary results in the hypersecretion of _____. This can result in infertility because of the inhibition of _____. This is often treated with a _____ agonist, such as _____ and _____.

21. Name 2 other high-yield conditions caused by hypersecreting pituitary adenomas.

22. List the direct catabolic effects of growth hormone.

23. List the direct and indirect anabolic effects of growth hormone.

24. _____ syndrome is a condition in which tissue production of somatomedins in response to growth hormone is lacking. Patients with the syndrome exhibit elevated circulating GH, but low levels of IGF-I.

25. What is the most common cause of acromegaly?

26. What drug can be used to suppress residual disease in acromegaly following surgery?

## TOPIC 2: THE THYROID

1. Sketch the sequence of hormones related to thyroid hormone regulation and include negative feedback in this description.

2. Indicate the key effects of thyroid hormone for the items in the first column.

| | T3/T4 Actions |
|---|---|
| Basal metabolic rate | |
| Nerves | |
| Bone | |
| Beta-receptors | |
| Cholesterol | |
| Muscle protein | |
| Growth hormone | |
| Gut motility | |

3. Indicate the key clinical signs seen in hypo- and hyperthyroidism for the following categories.

| | Hypo | Hyper |
|---|---|---|
| Basal metabolic rate | | |
| Nerves | | |
| Bone | | |
| Beta-receptors | | |
| Cholesterol | | |
| Muscle protein | | |
| Growth hormone | | |
| Gut motility | | |
| Other | | |

4. Why is hyperprolactinemia seen in some cases of hypothyroidism?

5. Name some of the clinical features of myxedema crisis.

6. List the 4 causes of hypothyroidism and indicate the most common cause.

7. Which HLA serotype is associated with Hashimoto's thyroiditis?

8. What autoantibodies are associated with Hashimoto's thyroiditis?

Endocrinology

9. Symptoms of hyperthyroidism may precede hypothyroidism in what diseases?

10. Biopsy of a thyroid gland damaged by giant cell thyroiditis (de Quervain's thyroiditis) would most likely show what feature?

11. In which form of thyroiditis does dense fibrosis replace the thyroid gland?

12. What long-term effect does hyperthyroidism have on muscle?

13. Name 4 conditions that can cause hyperthyroidism.

14. Besides hyperthyroidism, what 2 conditions are characteristic of Graves' disease?

15. Graves' disease usually involves what type of autoantibodies?

16. In toxic multinodular goiter, what causes the focal hyperfunctioning of follicular cells?

17. Benign, monoclonal tumors that form "cold nodules" on radioactive iodine uptake are typically what type of lesion?

18. Radiation therapy predisposes for what thyroid lesion?

19. What are characteristic histologic features of papillary thyroid carcinoma?

20. Which form of thyroid tumor has a particular propensity for metastasis via hematogenous spread to the bones or lungs?

21. Which thyroid tumor produces amyloid? What cell gives rise to this tumor?

22. Which types of MEN are associated with medullary thyroid carcinoma?

23. Where does the thyroglossal duct originate and what is its postnatal remnant called?

24. What is the most common location of ectopic thyroid tissue?

25. Name two other ventral outgrowths of foregut endoderm.

26. Where would a thyroglossal cyst most likely be found?

## TOPIC 3: THE PARATHYROIDS AND CALCIUM HOMEOSTASIS

1. Fill in the embryonic origins of the glandular tissue.

| Glandular Tissue | Pharyngeal Pouch Origin? | Migrates To? |
|---|---|---|
| Superior parathyroid | | |
| Inferior parathyroid | | |
| Parafollicular "C" cells | | |

2. Indicate the stimulus for the release of parathyroid hormone (PTH), and describe its actions on peripheral tissue.

3. Indicate the 2 sources for active vitamin D (calcitriol) and its primary physiologic effect.

4. Fill in the table below.

| Signs/Symptoms | Disease | Plasma $Ca^{2+}$ & Pi |
|---|---|---|
| ↑ QT interval; spasms; ↓ urine Pi; ↓ plasma PTH | | |
| | Pseudo-hypoparathyroidism | |
| ↓ QT interval; ↓ neuronal excitability; ↑ urine Pi | | |
| | Renal failure | |
| | | ↓ and ↓ |

5.  What is the most common cause of hypoparathyroidism?

6.  List 3 or more signs and symptoms of hypoparathyroidism.

7.  What causes pseudohypoparathyroidism?

8.  What chromosome defect causes DiGeorge's syndrome?

9.  A serum chloride-to-phosphate ratio greater than what number suggests hyperparathyroidism?

10. By what mechanism does chronic kidney disease cause secondary hyperparathyroidism?

## TOPIC 4: THE ADRENALS: STEROIDS AND CATECHOLAMINES

1. Fill in the functions and regulators of the regions of the adrenal gland.

| Glandular Region | Product(s)? | Regulated By? |
|---|---|---|
| Zona glomerulosa | | |
| Zona fasciculata | | |
| Zona reticularis | | |
| Medulla | | |

2. Where does the left and right adrenal vein drain?

3. Where does the left and right gonadal vein drain?

4. Fill in the table below for the important distinctions related to enzyme deficiencies in adrenal steroid synthesis. In all cases, cortisol is reduced, resulting in elevated ACTH and adrenal hyperplasia.

| Enzyme Deficiency | DOC | ALDO | Androgens | Renin | BP | Plasma K+ |
|---|---|---|---|---|---|---|
| 21-OH | | | | | | |
| 11β-OH | | | | | | |
| 17α-OH | | | | | | |

DOC = 11-deoxycorticosterone; ALDO = aldosterone

5. 21-hydroxylase deficiency produces what changes in functional steroid hormones?

6.  What adrenal enzyme deficiency accounts for 7% of adrenal enzyme deficiencies and causes increased androgens with virilization of female fetuses?

7.  Is there hypertension or hypotension in 21-hydroxylase deficiency?

    In 11β-hydroxylase deficiency?

8.  For the following, indicate the effects of cortisol.

    a.  Carbohydrates:

    b.  Fats:

    c.  Proteins:

    d.  Bone:

    e.  Phospholipase A2:

    f.  IL-2 production:

9.  Discuss the important permissive actions of cortisol and include any enzymes that may be involved.

10. Diagram the hypothalamic-pituitary-adrenal (HPA) axis.

11. Fill in the table below for the important hormonal alterations seen with adrenal cortex or HPA axis alterations.

| Condition | Cortisol | ACTH | DEX Suppression? | Pigmentation? |
|---|---|---|---|---|
| Addison's disease | | | | |
| Secondary hypocortisolism | | | | |
| Primary hypercortisolism | | | | |
| Cushing's disease | | | | |
| Ectopic ACTH | | | | |

DEX = dexamethasone

12. What is the most common cause of Cushing's syndrome?

13. "Buffalo hump" suggests what medical condition?

14. Cushing's disease is related to what type of tumor?

15. What are the typical etiologies of primary hypocortisolism (Addison's disease)?

16. What process would most likely cause an acute onset of adrenal insufficiency?

17. What parts of the adrenal glands atrophy in secondary hypocortisolism?

18. Fill in the table below for the important alterations associated with changes in aldosterone.

| Condition | ALDO | Renin | BP | Plasma K+ | Acid-Base | Edema? |
|---|---|---|---|---|---|---|
| Addison's | | | | | | |
| Conn's | | | | | | |
| Secondary hyper: renal artery stenosis | | | | | | |
| Secondary hyper: CHF, cirrhosis; nephrotic | | | | | | |

19. What is the most common cause of primary hyperaldosteronism (Conn's syndrome)?

20. How does renal artery stenosis cause secondary hyperaldosteronism?

21. Which species of bacteria is most likely to cause Waterhouse-Friderichsen syndrome?

22. What substances are pheochromocytomas likely to secrete?

23. Which urinary compounds are most important in the diagnosis of pheochromocytoma?

24. In general, the MEN syndromes are characterized by what problems? Which types are associated with pheochromocytoma?

25. MEN1 is caused by a loss of function mutation for the gene encoding what protein?

26. What are the 3 Ps of MEN1?

27. A pancreatic VIPoma seen in an MEN1 patient would likely produce what symptoms?

28. Mutation of the RET proto-oncogene can be seen in which forms of MEN?

29. Which form of thyroid cancer is associated with MEN2?

30. What is the most common extracranial malignancy of childhood?

31. What oncogene is amplified in neuroblastoma?

32. An abdominal neuroblastoma most likely arose from what site?

33. What is Kerner-Morrison syndrome?

34. Carcinoid syndrome is caused by secretion of what substance?

35. What urinary substance is characteristically increased in carcinoid syndrome?

## TOPIC 5: THE PANCREAS AND DIABETES

1. For the following islet cells, list the product and percentage of endocrine pancreas that each makes up.

| Islet Cell | Product? | % of Islet Cells? |
|---|---|---|
| Alpha | | |
| Beta | | |
| Delta | | |

2. What are the signal transduction pathways for insulin and glucagon?

3. Sketch the steps involved in the secretion of insulin, and indicate the compound that is co-released with it.

4. Fill in the table below for the important metabolic actions of insulin and glucagon.

| Hormone | Gly-S | Gly-P | Glu-neo | G6P | Plasma Glucose | HSL | ACC | Protein Synthesis |
|---|---|---|---|---|---|---|---|---|
| Insulin | | | | | | | | |
| Glucagon | | | | | | | | |

Gly-S = glycogen synthase; Gly-P = glycogen phosphorylase; Glu-neo = gluconeogenesis; G6P = glucose-6 phosphatase; HSL = hormone sensitive lipase; ACC = acetyl CoA carboxylase

5. Insulin increases the number of _____ transporters on skeletal muscle and adipose tissue. It also promotes the entry of the ion _____ into cells.

6. What is the leading cause of nontraumatic lower limb amputation?

7. Which HLA types are associated with type 1 diabetes mellitus?

8. What is the pathogenesis of diabetes mellitus type 2?

9. What substances create a diabetogenic effect in gestational diabetes?

10. What are some renal complications of diabetes?

11. What problems can be seen with diabetic retinopathy?

12. The neuropathy of diabetes mellitus is related to the increased intracellular concentration in neurons of what sugars or molecules closely related to sugars?

Endocrinology

13. What is the most common acute, life-threatening complication of type 1 diabetes mellitus?

14. Which serum ketones rise during diabetic ketoacidosis?

15. What are some common precipitating factors for diabetic ketoacidosis?

16. What characterizes the HONK state?

17. How is diabetic hyperosmolar nonketotic state treated?

18. What are the current diagnostic criteria for diabetes?

19. How is hemoglobin A1c produced in the diabetic patient?

20. With type 2 diabetics, how much weight loss is needed to improve insulin sensitivity and reduce postprandial hyperglycemia?

21. What condition would most likely be present in a diabetic patient who presented with diaphoresis, tremor, tachycardia, hunger, and altered mental status?

# NEPHROLOGY

## TOPIC 1: RENAL ANATOMY AND PHYSIOLOGY

1.  Name the 3 stages of embryonic kidney development and indicate which stage will form the definitive human kidney.

2.  When the mesonephric kidney degenerates, what does the cranial end of the mesonephric duct form in males?

3.  What structure begins the formation of the definitive human kidney?

4.  Where does the definitive human kidney initially develop?

5. The embryonic origin of the bladder and urethra is ———————————————.

6. Name 3 malformations evident in a stillborn infant that succumbed from bilateral renal agenesis (Potter sequence).

7. What vessel blocks the ascent of a horseshoe kidney?

8. In a newborn with a patent urachus, there will be abnormal drainage of urine from

   ———————————.

9. The 3 main anatomic regions of the kidney are ———————————————.

10. Which nephrons have short loops of Henle and which nephrons have long ones?

11. Name the 3 structures, in order, through which urine will pass to reach the ureter, beginning at the apex of a renal pyramid.

12. If Potter sequence develops from renal agenesis, what features are seen?

13. Failure of the allantois to obliterate embryologically can cause what problem?

14. Name and briefly describe the 4 basic renal processes.

15. About _____ of the body mass is water and its distribution is about _____ extracellular and _____ intracellular.

16. Four grams of inulin is infused into a patient, and the plasma concentration of inulin is 250 mg/ml after steady state has been achieved. What compartment is measured, and what is the volume of this compartment?

17. Complete the table below to denote the body compartment that each tracer measures.

| Tracer | Plasma | Extracellular | Total |
|---|---|---|---|
| $^{125}$I-albumin; Evan's blue dye; $^{51}$Cr red blood cell | | | |
| Inulin; mannitol; 22Na$^+$; sucrose | | | |
| Heavy water; tritiated water; urea; antipyrine | | | |

18. Under normal circumstances, _____ and _____ compounds are not filtered at the glomerular capillary.

19. Define glomerular filtration rate (GFR) and indicate the force producing it.

20. Write the equation for filtration fraction and indicate the variable it influences (directly related).

21. Using arrows, fill in the table below to indicate the effect sympathetic stimulation and angiotensin II have on renal function.

| | RPF | $P_{GC}$ | $P_{PC}$ | GRF | FF | $\pi_{PC}$ |
|---|---|---|---|---|---|---|
| Sympathetics (both but afferent > efferent) | | | | | | |
| Angiotensin II (efferent > afferent) | | | | | | |

RPF = renal plasma flow; $P_{GC}$ = pressure glomerular capillary; $P_{PC}$ = pressure peritubular capillary; GFR = glomerular filtration rate; FF = filtration fraction; $\pi_{PC}$ = oncotic pressure in the peritubular capillary

22. What is the important role of prostaglandins in the regulation of renal blood flow? Which over-the-counter compounds block prostaglandin production?

23. Write the equation for clearance. The clearance of which compound is a measure of GFR? Why is this compound a measure of GFR?

24. Plasma creatinine is used as a marker of renal function because _____.

25. The clearance of _____ is a measure of effective renal plasma flow, and it is utilized for this measurement because if the plasma concentration is low enough, all of it is _____.

26. Compound X is infused into a patient until it reaches a steady-state plasma concentration of 100 mg/dl. Once steady state is reached, the urine concentration of X is 2 mg/ml and urine flow is 1 ml/min. Inulin clearance is 100 ml/min. Given this, is there net secretion or reabsorption of X? What is the rate of this reabsorption or secretion, and is the clearance of X greater than, equal to, or less than GFR?

## TOPIC 2: ELECTROLYTES AND ACID-BASE DISORDERS

1. For the following solutes, indicate if the proximal tubule transport is: simple diffusion (SD), secondary active transport—symport ($2^\circ$ sym), secondary active transport—antiport ($2^\circ$ anti), or primary active transport ($1^\circ$), and indicate if this transport is across the luminal (L) or basolateral (BL) membrane.

| Glucose | AA | Ketones |
|---|---|---|
| $Na^+$–$H^+$ | $Na^+$–$K^+$ | $Na^+$–Pi |

AA = amino acids; Pi = phosphate

2. Discuss the steps involved in bicarbonate reabsorption across the luminal membrane of the proximal tubule.

3. Describe the effect on proximal tubular reabsorption of bicarbonate in the following conditions:

   Acidosis

   Alkalosis

   Administration of a carbonic anhydrase inhibitor

4. Discuss the renal consequences that occur when plasma glucose rises.

5. Indicate the tubular fluid-to-plasma concentration ratio (TF/P) (normal = 1) for the following solutes at the end of the proximal tubule. Write 1, >1, <1, or 0.

| | Glucose | Bicarbonate | $Na^+$ | $K^+$ | Cl- | Creatinine | Inulin |
|---|---|---|---|---|---|---|---|
| TF/P | | | | | | | |

6. The descending limb of the loop of Henle is permeable to _____ and relatively impermeable to _____.

7. Indicate the predominant transporter in the ascending thick limb of the loop of Henle (ATL) and the class of drugs that inhibit it.

8. The back diffusion of _____ from cells in ATL into the lumen drives the reabsorption of _____ and _____ in this region of the nephron.

9. The transporter in the distal tubule transports what 2 ions, and what class of drugs blocks this transporter?

10. Discuss the reabsorption of $Ca^{2+}$ in the distal tubule, what regulates it, and how it is impacted by thiazide diuretics.

11. _____ is a steroid hormone secreted from the adrenal cortex. It works on principal cells of nephron to increase _____ reabsorption and _____ secretion.

12. What are the 2 mechanisms of action of aldosterone on principal cells of the collecting duct?

Nephrology

13. Intercalated cells of the collecting duct play an important role in _____ regulation. They secrete _____ into the lumen, which in turn binds to _____
and/or _____ and is thus eliminated from the body. This process generates
_____. Aldosterone stimulates _____ secretion in these
cells; thus an excess of aldosterone causes an _____.

14. Principal cells contain receptors for the peptide hormone _____. This hormone causes
insertion of _____ in the luminal membrane.

15. Describe what stimulates the release of atrial natriuretic peptide (ANP) and indicate its effects on
the kidney.

16. List the 3 stimuli for renin release and the effects of renin.

Effects of renin:

17. List 4 important actions of angiotensin II.

(1)

(2)

(3)

(4)

18. List the 2 stimuli for the release of anti-diuretic hormone (ADH; also called arginine vasopressin, AVP).

19. Most of the body stores of $K^+$ are located in the _____ compartment.

20. Indicate whether the following conditions promote $K^+$ to shift into or out of cells.

    Acidosis _____

    Alkalosis _____

    Lysis of cells _____

    Beta-2 agonists _____

    Insulin _____

    Exercise _____

21. List 5 factors/conditions that increase $K^+$ secretion in the kidney.

    (1)

    (2)

    (3)

    (4)

    (5)

22. Fill in the table below.

| Acid/Base Disturbance | pH | Bicarbonate |
|---|---|---|
| Respiratory acidosis | | |
| | ↓ | ↓ |
| | ↑ | ↓ |
| Metabolic alkalosis | | |

23. Fill in the table below.

| Acid-Base Disturbance | Computation/Data Used to Diagnose the Condition |
|---|---|
| Acute (uncompensated) respiratory acidosis | |
| | Expected bicarbonate: 0.4 mEq/L * ↑ in $PCO_2$ |
| Metabolic acidosis | |
| | Expected bicarbonate: 0.2 mEq/L * ↓ in $PCO_2$ |
| Chronic (compensated) respiratory alkalosis | |
| Metabolic alkalosis | |
| Mixed disturbance | |
| Normal blood values | pH = 7.4; bicarbonate = 24 mEq/L; $PCO_2$ = 40 mmHg |

24. What is the normal anion gap and how is it calculated?

25. List the agents that cause an increased anion gap metabolic acidosis.

26. Complete the following table for renal tubular acidosis (RTA).

| | RTA Type I | RTA Type II | RTA Type IV |
|---|---|---|---|
| Fundamental dysfunction | | | |
| Urine pH | | | |
| Plasma K$^+$ | | | |
| Associated conditions | | | |

## TOPIC 3: NEPHRITIC AND NEPHROTIC SYNDROMES

1. What types of acellular and cellular casts can be present in urine?

2. Hyaline casts are composed of what protein?

3. Breakdown of cellular casts produces what type of cast as the next step?

4. A patient with nephrotic syndrome would be most likely to have _____ casts in the urine.

5. Red blood cell casts suggest damage to what renal structure?

6. Name 3 diseases that might be suggested by white blood cell casts.

7. Which features are characteristic of nephritic syndrome? Nephrotic syndrome?

8. Which bacteria are particularly likely to cause acute postinfectious glomerulonephritis?

9. What characteristic feature is seen on electron microscopy of glomeruli in acute poststreptococcal glomerulonephritis? Immunofluorescence?

10. Is the prognosis for acute poststreptococcal glomerulonephritis better for children or for adults?

11. The autoantibody of Goodpasture's syndrome is directed against what substance?

12. On immunofluorescence, what pattern is seen in Goodpasture's syndrome?

13. What is the outcome of most cases of rapidly progressive glomerulonephritis?

14. Rapidly progressive glomerulonephritis may occur in association with what diseases?

15. What findings are seen on light microscopy in rapidly progressive glomerulonephritis?

16. What medications are used to treat patients with rapidly progressive glomerulonephritis?

17. The most common cause of glomerulonephritis worldwide is _____.

18. What is seen on immunofluorescence of IgA nephropathy?

19. Membranoproliferative glomerulonephritis can occur secondary to what diseases?

20. Silver stain of a renal biopsy from a patient with membranoproliferative glomerulonephritis would likely show what distinctive feature?

21. If a person with membranoproliferative glomerulonephritis undergoes renal transplantation, what typically happens to the transplant?

Nephrology

22. What genetic mutation is associated with Alport syndrome?

23. When used in nephrotic syndrome, ACE inhibitors can help to control what disease manifestations?

24. Name several risk factors for membranous glomerulonephritis.

25. Light microscopy of silver-stained sections from a renal biopsy with membranous glomerulonephritis would show what distinctive feature?

26. What is the probable range of outcomes of membranous glomerulonephritis?

27. The most common cause of nephrotic syndrome in children is _____.

28. The most characteristic feature on electron microscopy of minimal change disease is _____.

29. In the United States, focal segmental glomerulosclerosis is most prevalent in what patient population?

30. Light microscopy of focal segmental glomerulosclerosis shows variable features with what range of appearance?

31. What are typical glomerular pathologies seen in diabetic renal disease?

32. Accumulation of amyloid deposits in glomeruli can produce what clinical syndrome?

# TOPIC 4: STONES, CANCERS, AND HEREDITARY DISORDERS

1. What features characterize the urine cytology in acute tubular necrosis?

2. What are the most common etiologies of acute tubular necrosis?

3. What are the most important organisms to cause pyelonephritis?

4. Urinalysis in pyelonephritis would be most likely to show what features?

5. What processes can cause tubulointerstitial nephritis?

6. What is the mechanism by which drugs can cause interstitial nephritis?

7. What is the most common cause of chronic drug-induced interstitial nephritis?

8. What processes can cause urate nephropathy?

9. The damage to the kidney in renal papillary necrosis is localized to which areas?

10. Why are fluids given in renal papillary necrosis?

11. The mechanism that causes diffuse cortical necrosis is: _____

_____.

12. Which bacterial species characteristically cause magnesium-ammonium phosphate stones?

13. Vitamin C abuse predisposes to what type of renal stones?

14. Cystine stones are related to a metabolic disorder involving what biochemical process?

15. What are the 2 most common presentations for nephrolithiasis?

16. A renal hamartoma composed of fat, smooth muscle, and blood vessels would most likely be associated with what disease?

17. Some risk factors for renal cell carcinoma are:

18. Renal cell carcinoma often reaches the heart by invading what structure?

19. Renal cell carcinomas can secrete a variety of hormones leading to what symptoms?

20. What are the components of the WAGR syndrome?

21. What 3 elements are seen in the histology of Wilms tumor?

22. The long-term survival of Wilms tumor patients can be how high?

23. What are the risk factors for transitional carcinoma?

24. The cysts of autosomal recessive polycystic kidney disease form in what structures?

25. Which genes are associated with adult (autosomal dominant) polycystic kidney disease?

26. What vascular disease is associated with autosomal dominant polycystic kidney disease?

27. Acquired polycystic kidney disease is seen in what patient population?

28. What processes can lead to pre-renal failure?

29. What cardiac condition can be caused by renal failure?

30. The impaired regulation of acid-base balance seen in renal failure is due to what process?

31. What endocrine functions of the kidney are disrupted by renal failure?

32. What is the underlying mechanism of pre-renal failure?

33. List some examples of acute intra-renal failure.

34. What are the 2 most common causes of chronic renal failure?

35. The hyperkalemia of chronic renal failure is initially compensated for by increased secretion of what hormone?

# TOPIC 5: DIURETICS

1. For each description below, identify the type of diuretic as CAI (carbonic anhydrase inhibitor), loop, thiazide, or $K^+$-sparing.

| Property | Diuretic |
|---|---|
| Causes hyperlipidemia | |
| Blocks $Na^+K^+ 2Cl^-$ pump | |
| Used in acute mountain sickness | |
| Hyperkalemic acidosis on overdose | |
| Causes ototoxicity | |
| Causes bicarbonaturia | |
| Used in female hirsutism | |
| Blocks $NA^+Cl^-$ pump | |

2. Identify whether each property below is for an ACEI, ARB, or both.

| Property | Drug |
|---|---|
| Chronic cough | |
| ↑ renin | |
| ↑ angiotensin II | |
| ↑ angiotensin I | |
| Hyperkalemia | |
| Angioedema | |
| Teratogenic | |
| ↓ aldosterone | |

Nephrology

# REPRODUCTIVE MEDICINE

## TOPIC 1: GAMETOGENESIS

1. When does spermatogenesis begin?


2. Similar to the cerebral circulation, the testes have a _____ barrier. Why is this important?


3. What cells form the blood-testis barrier? What germ cell is not protected by the barrier?


4. Diagram the basic sequence of spermatogenesis indicating whether each cell is diploid or haploid.


5. Diagram the basic sequence of folliculogenesis indicating whether each cell is diploid or haploid.

6.  Fill in the number of chromosomes (e.g., 23 or 46) and the complement of DNA (1N, 2N, 4N) in the nucleus of germ cells in the table below.

| | Karyotype |
|---|---|
| Spermatogonia | |
| Primary spermatocytes | |
| Secondary spermatocytes | |
| Spermatids | |
| Spermatozoa | |

7.  _____ is the ATPase protein associated with microtubules of the flagella and is necessary for normal motility.

8.  What is the acrosome of the sperm derived from? _____

9.  What is defective in sperm in Kartagener's syndrome? _____

10. What is a normal sperm count? _____

11. How many days are required for sperm maturation? _____

12. Where in the male does sperm mature? _____

13. Which presumptive gametes develop closest to the basement membrane of a seminiferous tubule?

14. Sketch the hypothalamic-pituitary-gonadal axis in men. Indicate the cells influenced by the pituitary hormones and what each cell secretes to provide negative feedback regulation.

15. Name 2 pituitary hormones that would be elevated in the event of castration.

16. Sketch the hypothalamic-pituitary-gonadal axis in women. Indicate the cells influenced by the pituitary hormones and what each cell secretes to provide negative feedback regulation.

17. In a woman, when does the first secondary oocyte appear? _____

18. In women, when does follicular atresia begin? _____

19. What stage of gametogenesis are all oocytes in at birth? _____

20. How many secondary oocytes are produced from a single primary oocyte? _____

21. At what arrested stage of gametogenesis is an ovulated oocyte? _____

22. What event immediately precedes the completion of meiosis II in women?

23. _____ stimulates the enzyme _____, which converts androgens into estrogens. This occurs in both the _____ and _____ cells.

24. What is the dominant hormone of the follicular phase, what cells secrete it, and what are the changes it evokes in the endometrium?

25. What is the dominant hormone of the luteal phase, what secretes it, and what are the changes it evokes in the endometrium?

26. Near mid-cycle, estradiol exerts a _____ feedback on the anterior pituitary, which induces a surge in _____ and _____, resulting in ovulation.

27. A 23-year-old woman is being evaluated for infertility. Her BMI is 32 and plasma glucose 160 mg/dL. Hirsutism is noted. She indicates a lack of a regular menstrual cycle. This patient likely has _____ syndrome. Her anterior pituitary hormones show an elevated _____ and a reduced _____.

28. Describe the hormonal changes and some key alterations experienced by women undergoing menopause.

29. What are some possible causes of anovulation?




30. Estrogen treatment for some of the symptoms of menopause often includes giving _____ to reduce the risk of _____ cancer.


31. Indicate the source of maternal hormones in the first, second, and third trimesters, and include the source of these hormones.

## TOPIC 2: FERTILIZATION AND EMBRYOGENESIS

1. What cell is formed at fertilization?

2. What is occurring during capacitation?

3. What must a capacitated sperm pierce for fertilization to occur?

4. On what day does implantation typically occur?

5. Name 2 risk factors for a tubal ectopic pregnancy.

6. Name 3 signs of a patient with an ectopic tubal pregnancy.

7. Name the 2 components of the blastocyst.

8. What cells produce human chorionic gonadotropin (hCG), and what is its function?

9. What 2 cell layers make up the embryonic disk in week 2?

10. What cells come in direct contact with fetal blood in the placenta?

11. What is specifically detected in the urine in a pregnancy test?

12. What might lower than normal levels of hCG indicate?

13. What might higher than normal levels of hCG indicate?

14. What germ layers are present in the embryo by week 3?

15. What is the name of the process that establishes the 3 germ layers?

16. Name the 3 germ layers.

17. What does a sacrococcygeal teratoma develop from?

18. In the list below, name the germ layer origin of the following structures: E for ectoderm, M for mesoderm, or EN for endoderm.

   (A)   Spleen

   (B)   Urinary epithelium

   (C)   Anterior pituitary

   (D)   Thymus

   (E)   Heart

   (F)   Notochord

   (G)   Tracheal epithelium

   (H)   Connective tissue

   (I)   Inner ear

   (J)   Liver parenchyma

   (K)   Lung epithelium

   (L)   Neural tube

   (M)   Submandibular glands

   (N)   Auditory tube

   (O)   Kidneys

   (P)   Lower vagina

   (Q)   Thyroid epithelium

19. Name 2 organ systems that develop in week 4.

# TOPIC 3: PREGNANCY

1. What is the most common cause of a spontaneous abortion in the first trimester?

2. What medication is used to treat stable ectopic pregnancies?

3. Spontaneous abortions in the second trimester can be due to what processes?

4. What is a common placental cause of painless vaginal bleeding? Painful vaginal bleeding?

5. What term is used when the umbilical cord runs over the inner cervical os?

6. The presence of what condition distinguishes eclampsia from preeclampsia?

7. What does the mnemonic in HELLP syndrome stand for?

8. A pregnant woman who develops preeclampsia at less than 20 weeks would be most likely to have what form of pregnancy?

9. What are potential causes of polyhydramnios? Oligohydramnios?

10. Describe the milk let-down reflex.

## TOPIC 4: NORMAL AND ABNORMAL DEVELOPMENT I

1.  List the 4 hormones/factors required for normal sexual differentiation in men and their basic action.

2.  _____ syndrome is a condition in which a genetic male exhibits the sexual external phenotype of a female at birth.

3.  Where are the testes found in androgen insensitivity syndrome? What would be the findings on pelvic examination?

4.  An abnormal opening of the urethra on the dorsal side of the penis is called _____.

5.  Uterine didelphys is due to a failure of fusion of what structures?

6.  Precocious puberty is defined to be the appearance of secondary sex characteristics before what age in girls?

    In boys?

7. What are possible causes of central precocious puberty?

8. Besides the congenital adrenal hyperplasias, what other conditions can cause peripheral precocious puberty?

9. What bone disease is associated with McCune-Albright syndrome?

## TOPIC 5: NORMAL AND ABNORMAL DEVELOPMENT II

1. What are 3 main categories of delayed puberty?

2. What changes in hormone levels are seen in hypergonadotropic hypogonadism?

3. Turner syndrome patients have an increased risk for what ovarian tumor?

4. What is the most common genetic composition for mixed gonadal dysgenesis?

5. What hormonal changes are seen in Klinefelter's syndrome?

6. Patients with 47, XYY have a 1-2% risk of what psychiatric disorder?

7. What hormonal changes are seen in androgen insensitivity syndrome?

8. What conditions can cause hypogonadotropic hypogonadism?

9. What is Mayer-Rokitansky-Küster-Hauser syndrome?

10. What endocrine changes are seen in polycystic ovary syndrome?

11. Considering the more common congenital adrenal hyperplasias, which have increased sex hormones? Decreased?

12. 5-α-reductase deficiency impairs the body's ability to convert _____ to _____.

## TOPIC 6: ANATOMY AND PHYSIOLOGY

1. Name the 3 anatomic positions of the uterus in the pelvis.

2. Name the 3 parts of the uterine tube.

3. What kind of epithelium lines the uterine tube? _____

4. What 3 ligaments hold the uterus in place in the pelvis?

5. What vessels course in the suspensory ligaments of the ovary? _____

6. Into what vein do the right and the left ovarian veins drain? _____

7. What structures are contained in the broad ligament? _____

8. What structures are contained in the cardinal ligaments?

9. What embryonic structure becomes the round ligament?

10. What different types of epithelium line the endocervix and the ectocervix?

11. What is the name of the cervical zone where cervical cancers commonly develop?

12. What muscle forms the pelvic floor?

13. What diaphragm is found in the perineum?

14. Name distinct structures that drain into the periaortic nodes, the hypogastric nodes, and the inguinal lymph nodes.

15. Fill in the nerves involved in male sexual reflexes and their actions.

| Event | Nerves Involved | Actions |
|---|---|---|
| Erection | | NO release and vascular engorgement |
| Emission | | Delivery of sperm and seminal fluid to prostatic urethra; secretion of lubricating glands |
| Ejaculation | | Climax; contraction of bulbospongiosus to expel sperm and seminal fluid through urethra |

16. Name a systemic cause of erectile dysfunction.

17. Name 2 types of medications that could cause erectile dysfunction.

18. What is the mechanism of action of sildenafil?

Reproductive Medicine

# TOPIC 7: FEMALE TRACT PATHOLOGY I

1. What virus is associated with vulvar intraepithelial neoplasia?

2. What is the most common form of invasive vulvar carcinoma? What are the less common forms?

3. What important difference is present between Paget's disease of the breast and Paget's disease of the vulva?

4. Vaginal squamous cell carcinoma typically occurs in what part of the vagina?

5. Clear cell adenocarcinoma of the vagina was historically associated with *in utero* exposure to what drug?

6. A polypoid grape-like soft tissue mass protruding from the vagina of a young girl is most likely what tumor?

7. Which 2 types of HPV are particularly likely to cause cervical cancer?

8. What is the progression in development of invasive cervical squamous cell carcinoma?

9. What term is used for a cervical squamous cell with a perinuclear halo?

10. Lymphatic spread from cervical cancer occurs to which nodes?

11. What conditions can cause increased risk of endometrial carcinoma related to increased estrogen exposure?

12. Endometrial carcinoma is also associated with what polyposis syndrome?

13. How is endometrial hyperplasia classified?

14. What is the most common tumor of the uterus? What is the associated histology?

15. At what site would a leiomyoma that causes menorrhagia most likely be located?

16. What term would be used to describe a uterine sarcoma that contains bone and cartilage?

17. What are common sites of endometriosis?

18. What process would most likely cause a small patch of blue discoloration on the serosal surface of the pelvic cavity?

19. Chocolate cysts of the ovaries are indicative of what condition?

20. High levels of what hormone can be generated by gestational trophoblastic disease?

21. From which parent does the genetic material of a complete mole derive from?

22. What is the risk of choriocarcinoma developing from a complete mole?

23. What karyotypes do partial moles have?

24. How common is fallopian tube carcinoma?

# TOPIC 8: FEMALE TRACT PATHOLOGY II

1.  What type of cyst would produce a deeply yellow, thick wall on cross-section of an ovary?

2.  How are ovarian cancers classified?

3.  What is the most common malignant ovarian tumor?

4.  What is a serum marker that can be used to monitor recurrence or response to therapy with cystadenocarcinoma?

5.  What tumor types are classified as germ cell tumors?

6.  What ovarian tumor is similar to male seminoma?

7.  Gonadal dysgenesis and Turner's syndrome are associated with an increased risk for which ovarian tumor?

8.  Elevation of what serum marker is characteristic of yolk sac tumors (endodermal sinus tumors)?

9.  What characteristic histologic feature is found in yolk sac tumors?

10. Elevations of what 2 serum markers are characteristic of embryonal carcinoma?

11. Choriocarcinoma arises from which 2 types of cells?

12. Which type of teratoma is usually benign in a female?

13. Struma ovarii is a monodermal teratoma of the ovary that produces what type of tissue?

14. What are the gonadal stromal tumors?

15. "Coffee-bean"–shaped secretory spaces suggest which gonadal stromal tumor?

16. Sertoli–Leydig cell tumors can produce what hormones?

17. A Krukenberg tumor is a metastatic tumor to the ovary most commonly from what source?

# TOPIC 9: BREAST ANATOMY AND PATHOLOGY

1. What is the embryonic germ layer origin of breast tissue? _____

2. At puberty, what causes glandular proliferation of breast tissue? _____

3. What kind of ducts drain into the area of the nipple? _____

4. What does the breast produce immediately postpartum? _____

5. Which bacteria commonly cause acute mastitis?

6. Mammary duct ectasia most frequently occurs in what patient population?

7. Fat necrosis can cause calcifications in the breast that suggest what disease process?

8. What are some benign breast diseases?

9. What is the most common breast disorder in premenopausal women?

10. What would papillary proliferation of ductal epithelium seen in fibrocystic disease be called?

11. What is the most commonly diagnosed breast mass in young women?

12. Is cystosarcoma phyllodes a benign or a malignant tumor?

13. Clear, unilateral spontaneous nipple discharge from a single duct suggests what benign breast disease?

14. What are some important breast cancer risk factors?

15. Distinguish between BRCA1 and BRCA2.

16. Which quadrant of the breast has the highest frequency of breast cancer?

17. When a breast mass becomes "fixed," what does this suggest about where it has spread?

18. What type of mass does invasive lobular carcinoma usually produce?

19. What part of the breast does Paget's disease usually involve?

20. A breast duct containing a duct epithelial proliferation with cheesy necrotic tissue is likely to be what? _____

21. A breast cancer with sheets of large, pleomorphic cells showing lymphocytic infiltration would most likely be what type? _____

22. What does a "peau d'orange" appearance of a breast suggest?

23. What medication is an estrogen-receptor antagonist that is useful in breast cancer therapy?

## TOPIC 10: MALE TRACT PATHOLOGY

1. What term is used when the prepuce cannot be retracted over the glans penis?

2. Squamous cell carcinoma of the penis in men is most likely to be related to what viruses?

3. What is the most common cause of acute prostatitis? ⎯⎯⎯⎯⎯⎯⎯⎯⎯⎯⎯⎯⎯

4. What type of drug can relax the smooth muscle in the prostate and bladder neck to partially compensate for poor urine flow in patients with benign prostatic hyperplasia?

5. In what part of the prostate do most prostatic carcinomas arise? ⎯⎯⎯⎯⎯⎯⎯⎯⎯⎯⎯

6. Are prostate metastases to bone usually blastic or lytic? ⎯⎯⎯⎯⎯⎯⎯⎯

7. A football player who experiences sudden, excruciating testicular pain on one side after being tackled might have what condition? ⎯⎯⎯⎯⎯⎯⎯⎯⎯⎯⎯

8. What causes hydrocele?

9. Dilations of the testicular vein tributaries in the pampiniform plexus can produce what condition?

10. Which testicular tumor is unusual in that it contains cells derived from ectoderm, mesoderm, and endoderm?

11. What tumor markers are useful in seminoma?

12. What percentage of embryonal carcinomas of the testes have metastasized at the time of diagnosis?

13. What extratesticular manifestation may be caused by choriocarcinoma of the testes?

14. In what male patient population is yolk sac tumor seen?

15. When teratoma in testes is compared to teratoma in ovaries, which is more commonly malignant?

16. What is the most common testicular cancer in elderly men?

17. What percentage of pre-pubertal boys experience gynecomastia?

# TOPIC 11: SEX HORMONE PHARMACOLOGY

1.  The key difference between tamoxifen and raloxifene occurs on what organ?


2.  What drug is used to stimulate ovulation in the treatment of infertility?


3.  List the drug that matches the description below.

| Property | Drug |
|---|---|
| Relax uterus | |
| Aromatase inhibitor | |
| 5-α-reductase inhibitor | |
| Blocks testosterone receptors | |
| GnRH analog | |
| PGE₁ analog for erectile dysfunction | |

# TOPIC 12: SEXUALLY TRANSMITTED INFECTIONS

1. Add the symptoms, site of latency, and treatment for HSV-1 and HSV-2.

| Virus | Symptoms | Site of Latency | Treatment |
|-------|----------|-----------------|-----------|
| HSV-1 | | | |
| HSV-2 | | | |

2. Name the diagnostic cell forms found in herpesvirus infections.

3. Visible cauliflower lesions due to HPV are most commonly due to which 2 viral serotypes?

4. Genital cancers, including cervical cancer, are most commonly due to which 2 (or 4) serotypes? List 2 if possible.

5. List the causative agent, Gram stain reaction, and shape of syphilis.

6. List at least 1 symptom for each stage of syphilis.

| Stage of Syphilis | Symptom(s) |
|-------------------|------------|
| Primary | |
| Secondary | |
| Latent | |

Reproductive Medicine

7. List the screening and confirmatory tests for syphilis.


8. Place an "X" next to each symptom that occurs in congenital syphilis. If you can, list the congenital diseases with which the other symptoms are observed.

| Symptoms | Congenital Syphilis |
|---|---|
| Cataracts | |
| Saddle nose | |
| Snuffles | |
| Blueberry muffin baby (thrombocytic purpura) | |
| PDA | |
| 8th cranial nerve damage | |
| Hydrops fetalis | |

9. For each of the following statements, place a "T" if the statement applies to gonorrhea or "F" if the statement does not apply to gonorrhea.

- Causes urethritis in men
- Does not lead to infertility in women
- Is usually asymptomatic in women
- Can cause Fitz-Hugh-Curtis syndrome
- Causes an ulcerative lesion on the genitals
- Gram-negative diplococci on urethral Gram stain


10. Name the special culture media used to isolate *Neisseria gonorrhoeae*.

—————————————

Name the treatment for *Neisseria gonorrhoeae*. ———————————————

11. Fill in the blank with a > or <.

    *Chlamydia trachomatis* serotypes D–K are _____ common than *Neisseria gonorrhoeae*.

    Name the treatment for *Chlamydia trachomatis* serotypes D–K. _____

12. List the differential diagnosis for bacterial vaginosis. (list 3)

13. Name the treatment for vaginitis. _____

14. List the Gram reaction and shape for *Haemophilus ducreyi*. _____

    Discuss the diagnosis of *(H) ducreyi*.

15. List the serotypes of *Chlamydia trachomatis* that are associated with LGV.